TRUTH
about

BREAKING UP, MAKING UP, & MOVING ON

CHAD EASTHAM

THOMAS NELSON
Since 1798

NASHVILLE   DALLAS   MEXICO CITY   RIO DE JANEIRO

© 2013 by Chad Eastham

All rights reserved. No portion of this book may be reproduced, stored in a retrieval system, or transmitted in any form or by any means—electronic, mechanical, photocopy, recording, scanning, or other—except for brief quotations in critical reviews or articles, without the prior written permission of the publisher.

Published in Nashville, Tennessee, by Thomas Nelson. Thomas Nelson is a registered trademark of Thomas Nelson, Inc.

Original illustrations by James A. Phinney.

Thomas Nelson, Inc., titles may be purchased in bulk for educational, business, fundraising, or sales promotional use. For information, please e-mail SpecialMarkets@ ThomasNelson.com.

Unless otherwise noted, Scripture quotations are taken from HOLY BIBLE: NEW INTERNATIONAL VERSION®. © 1973, 1978, 1984 by International Bible Society. Used by permission of Zondervan Publishing House. All rights reserved. Scripture quotations marked NKJV are taken from THE NEW KING JAMES VERSION. © 1982 by Thomas Nelson, Inc. Used by permission. All rights reserved. Scripture quotations marked ESV are taken from THE ENGLISH STANDARD VERSION. © 2001 by Crossway Bibles, a division of Good News Publishers.

Library of Congress Cataloging-in-Publication Data

Eastham, Chad, 1980–
The truth about breaking up, making up, and moving on / by Chad Eastham.
p. cm.
ISBN 978-1-4003-2115-5 (pbk.)
1. Dating (Social customs)—Juvenile literature. 2. Dating (Social customs)—Religious aspects—Christianity—Juvenile literature.
3. Interpersonal relations in adolescence—Juvenile literature.
4. Separation (Psychology)—Juvenile literature. 5. Love—Juvenile literature. I. Title.
HQ801.E274 2013
306.73—dc23   2012032794

Printed in the United States of America

13 14 15 16 17 QG 6 5 4 3 2 1

To anyone reading this who has ever felt disheartened and confused, hurt or lost . . . you are not alone. You are surrounded by countless multitudes of people everywhere who are just like you. Just like us. But you don't have to stay confused or lost or in pain. We might forget this sometimes—or may not know at all. But there is nothing in your life, no matter how difficult or painful, that cannot be turned into something very beautiful. So please, have lots of hope . . . and this book is for you.

> So we do not lose heart. Though our outer self is wasting away, our inner self is being renewed day by day. For this light momentary affliction is preparing for us an eternal weight of glory beyond all comparison, as we look not to the things that are seen but to the things that are unseen.
>
> —2 Corinthians 4:16–18 ESV

CONTENTS

Contents

Part 4: Moving On

INTRODUCTION

Some Bad Things . . . Aren't

I'M TIRED OF THE SAME ADVICE

S tarting a book by talking about yourself probably isn't the most effective way to capture a reader, and I know this. I'm terribly sorry. But I decided to write this book a little differently because of a single thought that kept tapping on my brain . . . rudely, since I was having coffee on my porch that morning. The thought was:

This doesn't work.

I was thinking about a lot of things at that moment, really, and I mean a lot of things. Like the way squirrels in my front yard won't play with me. But more serious stuff too. Like the way we talk about life—our own relationships, our feelings, and our deepest insecurities. I look at charts and data and education initiatives, not to mention Christian culture, the trendy youth group names and popular fads, the applied psychology of teen social issues, and other things more boring than this list . . . and it just popped up, over and over, tapping at my brain: *this doesn't work*. And here is why I thought this odd, vague, not-yet-explained phrase . . . because it doesn't. It needs to change. The whole conversation needs to change. Most importantly . . . we need to change.

Figuring It Out

I have developed a thing for front porches in the last couple of years. And I love my front porch. When I work from home, I'm pretty much in my office or on the porch. In my front yard, there are these two giant old trees, which help the porch vibe, obviously, with a forty-foot-tall canopy. It has a very Jurassic Parky vibe, but without dinosaurs. Also, most people on my street are friendly, and I don't live on an island.

I sit on the porch any morning I'm at home and do a little relaxing—reading, reflecting, maybe praying, and just taking a few moments to wake up my mind peacefully. (Coffee also helps.) I watch these two little squirrels chase each other around the yard. I also have a hammock I spend a lot of time in—mostly just because hammocks are awesome and people don't have to explain why they have them.

For me, being outside in any way is a good reminder of many things—one is that not everything is air-conditioned.

And another is that, in fact, I live on a planet that is zipping through space at over 66,700 miles an hour, spinning in a circle at roughly 1,000 miles an hour. (NASA nerds like me, anyone?) All that is to say that I've thought through a lot of things on that front porch, watching squirrels usually. Here are a few . . .

OUT OF TOUCH

Sometimes I'm really out of touch, and maybe a lot of us are. All the distractions in a day—of the facespace and quick-paced tweeted world we live in—can keep me from really spending time on the important things. When I was growing up, people didn't tell me to slow down, to do less, to be calmer, or to practice being content. In fact, people told me to do the opposite: be involved, challenge myself, stay busy, push through the pain, chase after my goals, swing for the fences, do more, make more, go all out. But you wanna know something? When it comes to dealing with the hard stuff in life, it's the slowing down and remembering the basics that are most important. Also, all of those other words sound exhausting. Where's a hammock when you need one?

PAIN

There are odd things in life, and one of them is pain. The odd thing about pain is this: you can't avoid it. You just can't. Maybe if you lived in a sealed room your whole life you could, but that would be lonely and cause you emotional pain, and it might mean you've been kidnapped, so . . . just don't live in sealed rooms. Also . . . you can't avoid pain.

LIFE IS AMAZING

The hard stuff really is part of the good stuff. I do believe this is true, or at least it can be if we are willing to learn from the hard stuff. I mean, as little kids we learn that eating our broccoli means we can get dessert, while finger painting on the living room wall leads to less tasty consequences. In the same way, as we grow older we learn from the difficult experiences in life—and some of those experiences involve relationships.

> The hard stuff really is part of the good stuff. ←

The reason I can write a book about difficult things is because difficulty is temporary. Things don't have to stay difficult. Also, the best parts of life can't be separated from the hardest parts of life. And don't forget to enjoy simple stuff like . . . being alive, which in itself is amazing news. For me, personally, it means I'm not dead, and I'm a fan of that. Optimism can start small, ya know?

Life is, in fact, amazing. It's also messy, uncertain, and really crazy difficult too. And my point about pain is this: we think pain is terrible, and so did I for most of my life . . . but it's not. We treat pain and struggle like a disease that we have to get rid of quickly. But pain isn't necessarily bad; it's just painful. It has benefits too. Pain provides a chance for us to learn from our experiences and mistakes and to grow and change for the better. Struggles, failures, heartaches, and disappointments will teach us some of the most important lessons we can ever learn in life. The wisest people seem to look back on the painful and confusing times as a great gift. That's a secret we all need to learn—to see the tough times as opportunities. They can make you a better person, and you can even learn to be grateful for them. And trust me, if I had read that sentence just a few years ago, I would have laughed, rolled my eyes, and been annoyed at me. But now I'm saying it to you, and I'm saying it because it's true; it really is.

While I'm sure you were really excited about the squirrel-morning-coffee-peace retreats I was talking about earlier, my porch is also the place where I decided to write this book differently. We see so much struggle and confusion and pain in life and in relationships that we think it's normal, but this is a lie. It doesn't have to be that way.

I've received some seven thousand letters from young people in the last couple of years. And I can't tell you how many thousands of those letters were from teens asking me to *tell* them the answer to a problem. I can, however, tell you exactly how many teens have asked me *how to figure out* the answer to a problem. Zero. Not a one. This is significant because we don't just need the *answers* to our questions. We need to learn *how to find out* the answers to our questions.

That's why this book isn't easy—because it's not about getting lollipop answers to life's tough problems. You need more than that. I don't want you to depend on books like this for answers. I would rather you learn how to answer life's questions for yourself—and luckily you can do this. This might put me out of a writing job, but if people were happier then I'd gladly call it a fair trade.

THE FORMULA

There's a pretty easy, not-so-great, and generic formula for relationship books, in case you wanted to know. If you look for it, even in teen books, you can probably figure it out for yourself. The basic strategy is to give simple, easy-to-digest, snappy answers that make people feel better. It's often a pep talk in paperback, which is cool if you are looking for a pep talk—but not if you're looking to actually learn something, if you know what I mean.

Yes, it's important to know how to break up (thank you, books that provide basics), but it's just as important to know how to heal from that broken relationship. Because sometimes buying a new outfit, or planning a night out with friends, or focusing on your grades won't help you process the pain of a breakup. But instead, if you try to understand what happened and *why*, you can use your experiences to become a better person. Because you are quite capable, quite able, and quite brilliant, actually, and I'll prove it.

IT's NOT JUST ABOUT BREAKUPS

Sometimes life is overwhelming. Yes, there is gross and bad stuff—we get it. We hurt people, we get hurt by people, we have amazing happiness, and we have gigantic heartache. And if you picked up this book, the odds are that you are less interested in adorable puppy picture books, and you probably have some unpleasant things you are trying to make sense of. So while this book talks a lot about relationships and breakups, it's not really just about breakups. Luckily, the principles are the same for dealing with a lot of the tough things in life.

A SECRET

I have a secret for you . . . and I'll whisper it so I don't embarrass anyone: *you have a lot more control over your life than you think.*

In case you don't believe that now, I hope you will by the end of this book. You are not powerless in the whirlwind of life. Until you realize you aren't powerless, however, you will be a victim to every storm in life. And guess what? There are always storms on the horizon, storms like broken hearts, losing friends, loneliness, suffering, rejection, or birds pooping on you. You know . . . stuff like that. But you can be *prepared* for the storms, and I think this book will help. Kind of like an emergency road kit for life, or something like that.

You have *a lot* more control over your life than you think.

An Opposite Secret

Here's another secret for you: *you have a lot less control over your life than you think.*

But, Chad, you just said . . . I know, but oddly enough, this is also true. I used to think it was just the really smart people who were able to figure out the secrets to life, but now I don't. I think maybe the smart people just discovered the difference between what they actually *can* control and what they *cannot*. Maybe that's the "sweet spot" in life—focusing on the stuff you can do something about and not worrying about the other stuff.

This book is not about breakups. I mean, it is . . . but it isn't. For sure we will deal with breakups plenty. But this book is about helping you figure out *how* to figure things out. If you know anything about me (not that you need to), then you'll know that I don't like telling people what to do, or only giving them simple answers to life's complexities. And that's good news for you, because just giving you the answers won't help you. It's like math . . . kind of. Someone giving you the answer to a math question doesn't teach you math; You won't know how to answer the next math question. You won't understand *how* the math works.

Yes, you can still find answers here; there are plenty in this book. But there's a lot more to it than just how to dump someone, how to get over being dumped, and how to move on. This book is about understanding people, understanding yourself, and asking more questions.

These are the things you *can* control, and they are the things that matter. It will make a difference in your life too. It just starts with a little willingness and a little hope—which, since you had the nerve to pick up a book and learn a little, I'm betting you already have.

I promise you this: You can be happy, and clear, and ready for the future. You can get past heartache and hardship. You can have a healthy, happy, amazing life. Because your life belongs to you—and you matter. A lot.

—Chad

{ Hey! Let's Break Up }

chapter

SUPER SURE
IT'S LOVE?

{
Love: a virtue representing all of
human kindness, compassion, and
affection.

—*Merriam-Webster*[1]
}

{
To be loved is to be known, deeply,
and we all want to be loved.

—chad
}

THIS ABSOLUTELY MUST BE LOVE . . . MAYBE

Then you are a guy just starting college, already over-whelmed by everything new, you don't expect to run smack-dab into *her* the first week. *Her.* She was absolutely gorgeous, and I mean truly stunning, with crazy blue eyes, a wowing smile, and a super-awesome-looking face. Her name was Jen, but my brain immediately nicknamed her *dream girl*. (Also, ahead of time, this isn't *The Notebook* . . . sorry.) When

I met her, Jen had on running shorts and a beat–up college T-shirt, with a pencil between her teeth. I don't think the pencil was there permanently—probably she was just studying. Of course, she was even prettier because she laughed a lot, and the only wrinkles on her face were in the corners of her eyes, the kind people get from smiling, which are the best wrinkles, in my opinion. Not only was Jen breathtakingly stunning (and still is), but she was also really smart. And she turned out to be really, really nice to talk to. She was super friendly to me, and all I did was be kind of quiet and try not to look like an idiot barely keeping it together. I remember thinking, *Wow, there really are girls like this in the world, even at my college, and right in front of me. They're classy and beautiful and fun and mature, all at the same time.* Then I thought, *Well . . . that's pretty awful news.*

Okay . . . to make sense of that odd thought, here was my next thought:

Okay, self, now you know there are girls like this in the world, which is terrible information to know. Because someone will get to date this girl and get looked at all sweet by her, kiss her, and probably marry her. Some guy will get to smell her and hug her and stare at her whenever he wants. Here's the bad news, self: she can pick anyone she wants, ANYONE. She'll probably get all wooed by some smart, rich, dumbface, handsome, millionaire guy who doesn't care about money but has a lot of it. He'll probably have a private plane that goes to his private island that probably has dolphins. This means that Jen, on top of being happy and smart and pretty and sweet, will most likely get to own and name and play with . . . pet dolphins. You can't

4

compete with *dolphins*. On top of this, she'll probably tell this future jerk how special he is and brag about him to everyone at cool parties in neato places near the ocean. She'll probably even believe this jerk is special, but only because he most likely is special, and he's probably a jerk because he's not me.

Shortly after these punch-yourself-in-the-face thoughts, one of my friends decided to be extra cruel by telling me that Jen was saying nice things about me. A mean joke, most likely, I thought, so you can imagine my surprise when it turned out not to be a joke.

Jen did think I was nice and interesting, and this confused me greatly. Somehow, though, Jen and I hit it off. In fact, we hung out a handful of times and went on a few dates. We put futon chairs onto the roof of my dorm one night to watch a rare meteor shower, where we stared up at the sky all night and talked about life. It was an awesome night, actually. An incredible and beautiful girl just had a great time with me (which can greatly enhance a boy's self-esteem). But later, as I walked Jen back to her place on campus, that's when it got weird. She had a little look in her eye, and I kinda thought there was a kiss somewhere behind that look, maybe, lurking a little, or probably just me hoping. Because here was my inner monologue at that moment:

You did it, buddy. You didn't screw up. Good job, self. Now she's letting me walk her home. This is good. Okay, now wait. She's smiling at me and touching my hand. There's her door. She's slowing down. Wait, she touched my hand again. Accident? Messing with me? There's no way this girl wants me to actually touch her back. Why are her lips so amazing right now? Okay, wait . . . does she want me to kiss her? If I kiss her, and she lets me, I'm gonna freak out. There's no way she actually wants me to kiss her. But why is she smiling at me so much, then? Okay, self, according to all the movies I've seen in life, this is a scene where a girl might let a guy kiss her. Man, this is gonna be terrible if she . . . okay, wait . . . she's telling me now how much fun she had, and she's not backing away. Do it, idiot, just do it. Dude, listen to ME, it's YOU! Go, man! Move lips forward, take look of fear off face. Okay, here we go . . . this will probably end horribly . . .

Then I did it. I kissed her—the wowing, stunning college girl I never thought would even look at me. And she kissed me back. And I mean . . . it was a *really* nice kiss. The kind you see in movies, but without the music and film crew around. I started walking home in a daze, processing the new information about a world where a girl like that kissed me. Then . . . it happened. I felt it. It felt like . . . nothing.

Wait, what? . . . *nothing?* No fireworks, no soft music in the background. In all honesty . . . I just didn't feel what I was expecting to feel. And you know what? That's the stupidest feeling I might have ever had. Also, one of the most confusing. I thought I must be defective as a human being and a male, because who isn't deeply in love after *that* moment with *that* girl? That would be you, Chad, you idiot.

Here's the thing, though: I liked Jen a lot. I thought I liked her romantically, and I pictured what it would be like with her in a relationship and loved the idea. Plus, I couldn't believe she thought I was interesting enough to spend time with me, much less let me kiss her. For several days after that, I just sat and thought, which was important, because apparently my brain was broken, very damaged or defective, and needed fixing.

Fast-forward a little to what I know about it now: while I didn't understand it at the time—and it's weird to admit this on paper—I really had idealized Jen. (You've probably already figured that out.) The thing is, in the story in my mind, I made Jen out to be perfect, and that wasn't fair to her. In reality, I was being selfish, but maybe not in the "traditional" selfish way. I wasn't looking at Jen for who she really was; I was using her to show how important I must be. How could I not be important if a girl like that liked me, right? I really didn't mean to do that; I was just young and didn't know a better way of thinking. I've never really apologized to her for that specifically, mostly because I didn't know how to apologize for my brain not working. I can't see girls being cool with . . . "Hey, sorry about my brain not working right; that thing is nuts sometimes. I know I might have confused you, but my brain confused me too. Anyhoo . . . just letting you know that was why! Hugs!" I mean, I'd be willing to try it once . . . but just for the story, really.

To my benefit, Jen and I stayed friends. It was actually fine after a couple of weeks. Mostly because she's awesome and is cool enough not to hold grudges about my confusion. It made me respect her more in the bigger picture. And now, I think it's insane that I only looked at her with the romance goggles, and I did this from the instant I saw her. To be blunt with myself, I didn't really see her at all. I saw who I wanted her to be *for me*.

I'll bet I'm not alone in that either. I think a lot of us make that mistake.

In Love with Love

In hindsight, my real problem with Jen wasn't a problem with Jen at all. It was a problem with me. I wasn't in love; I was in love with being in love. Maybe you've done this too. Most people do this at least once, or a thousand times.

Why? Why do we do this? And how do we know when we are really in love . . . and not just in love with love? How do we know what love really is?

LOVE IS . . .

Love. We need it to live, just like we need air and food. Love connects human beings, and being connected—to God, to one another—is why we are here. Love is the best tool we have on earth. The best moments in life always seem to include other people, and usually it's us loving and caring and experiencing life with one another. At least those are my best memories in life so far.

> { Love is our true destiny. We do not find the meaning of life by ourselves alone—we find it with another.
> —Thomas Merton }

Love and romantic love are not the same, by the way. I think we should paint this on a wall a hundred feet high to remind ourselves. Romantic love is only a tiny, minuscule fraction of what *love* encompasses. If *romantic love* were a drop of water, the ocean it fell into would be the rest of love. But yes, for our purposes, people are mostly concerned with the romantic understanding of love. So let's talk about it. How do you know if it's really love? Because sometimes, as Marybeth mentions in her letter, love can be a pretty hard thing to make sense of:

Chad,

I had this boyfriend named Brent. I thought I loved him, and he said he loved me. But he would completely smother, control, and disrespect me. If I didn't answer his texts or his calls right away, he'd start blowing up at me or even come over. If I didn't pay for his meals, he'd say I was after his money, even though we only ordered off the dollar menus! He would say, "Why don't you wear short shorts, miniskirts, and string bikinis?" I told him it's because I'm modest, and I didn't like him saying this, but then he would get angry. How do you ever know if you are in love?

—Marybeth

To be clear, Marybeth is asking about love, but she's describing the opposite of love. This is probably confusing to someone reading her letter and even more confusing for Marybeth. *Love* is probably one of the most misused words in the history of . . . well, history. Why do people describe *fear* and call it *love*? Why do they describe confusion, control, disrespect, and heartache, yet call it love? No wonder life can be so confusing, especially as a teenager.

> Love is probably one of the most misused words in the history of . . . well, history.

9

So how do you know real love when you come across it? Well, for starters, let's look at a different letter. This actually *is* a love letter, even though it's only a few sentences long. And . . . it's different. It's from a young man writing on May 12, 1869, to a girl he intended to marry one day, expressing one way he thought about her:

> *Out of the depths of my happy heart wells a great tide of love and prayer for this priceless treasure [Olivia] that is confided to my lifelong keeping. You cannot see its intangible waves as they flow toward you, darling, but in these lines you will hear, as it were, the distant beating of its surf.*
>
> —Mark Twain to Olivia Langdon,
> his future wife

Can you see the difference in how they view love? Marybeth's letter is filled with fear and confusion and stress, but the other shows gratitude and humility and selflessness. Guess which relationship I'd bet on? I mean . . .

LOVE'S IMPULSIVE COUSIN

Sometimes people in love . . . aren't. They just aren't. Meet *infatuation*, the impulsive and loud cousin of love. Infatuation looks like love, smells like love, dresses like love, but it is *not* love. Emphasis on *not*. So let's first be clear about what it is then:

Infatuation is the state of being completely carried away by unreasoned passion or love. It "expresses the headlong libidinal attraction" of addictive love. Usually, one is inspired with an intense but short-lived passion or admiration for someone.[2]

Infatuation isn't wrong, by the way. It almost always exists in the beginning stage of love. It's actually there for a reason—a good one, potentially. Here's why: when you are first interested in someone, infatuation allows you to look past people's small imperfections, which is important to do in order to want to get to know them more. There's nothing wrong with thinking highly of people, unless it's not accurate, and then it's, well . . . not accurate. I think when people truly fall in love, the infatuation fades away and is replaced with a deeper, more realistic, and less fantasized version of love. In real love, no one is perfect or idealized; instead, a person is appreciated and understood for exactly who he or she is.

Infatuation—to put it simply—makes people's brains go a little bit crazy. In fact, left to its own neurotic devices, and without proper boundaries and guidance, the brain of an infatuated person very much resembles that of a drug addict.

It's not infatuation that's so addictive; rather, it's the chemicals (like dopamine and serotonin and oxytocin) our brains produce when we are infatuated that people get addicted to. Infatuation happens quickly. Simply

> The brain of an infatuated person very much resembles that of a drug addict.

put, it's an overreaction to someone, when you don't have enough real facts yet to validate your strong feelings. Three areas of your brain swing into action: the *right ventral tegmental region*, the *medial caudate nucleus*, and the *nucleus accumbens*. The chemicals produced by these three areas work together to shorten your attention span, cause short-term memory loss, and impact your goal-oriented behavior. You get an adrenaline rush, your heart rate goes up, you have trouble focusing, and your thoughts can become fixated on the other person. In other words, your judgment becomes impaired. So it's easy to see why people feel overwhelmed by their feelings in a relationship. And when you understand *why* something happens, it changes everything.[3]

> Love is patient, love is kind. It does not envy, it does not boast, it is not proud. It is not rude, it is not self-seeking, it is not easily angered, it keeps no record of wrongs. Love does not delight in evil but rejoices with the truth. It always protects, always trusts, always hopes, always perseveres. Love never fails.
> —1 Corinthians 13:4–8

While real love is patient, trusting, caring, gentle, pure, and not jealous, infatuation gets carried away by passion and leaves reasoning and thinking in the trash. Infatuation, after all, is like a drug that just happens to be legal.

U R Simply Not Right—4 Me

It's really difficult the moment you realize that someone just isn't "the right person for you," especially when you really thought he or she was. It can be hard to change the direction of a relationship when your mind has created a slightly different reality than the one that is currently smacking you in the face. Here's something you should know: the ability to start putting the childish version of love behind you and start looking at things more clearly and more truthfully is critical for life. It's part of growing up, and it makes your brain grow up too. There are many lessons to be learned about love. And one of the greatest of them is that infatuation is not the same as love. It never has been. It never will be.

The Love Connection

Love is connection. Our lives—our joy, imagination, and yes, relationships—are shaped by love or the absence of it. We need to be connected to other people, period. We need to be cared about and known by other human beings, on a deeply personal level. We also need to give this same deep sense of caring to others.

{ I have found that to love and to be loved is the most empowering and exhilarating of all human emotions.
—Jane Goodall }

Growing up, I didn't really understand much about God or the Bible, even when I tried. People at church told me that God is love. To be honest, it was hard for me to connect that idea with my everyday life. I didn't know what to do with "God is love"[4] when I was sitting around my room on a Thursday night. What I did know was that I liked having friends, and I liked it when girls were nice to me, along with some other basic human likes and whatnot. It seemed logical that if a pretty girl liked me, and she was liked by a lot of other people . . . then maybe, by default or something like that, those other people might like me too. I wasn't even really looking for true love. I was looking for people who might like me, or at least not hate me. It's not fun when people hate you and don't love you, in my experience anyway.

Now . . . it's different, and I don't really think that way anymore. I have learned more about what the word *love* can mean since then, whether I meant to or not. I didn't always like the answers people gave me about God either, because they seemed . . . small. So I had to go and look for myself— and I still do—and it's one of the best decisions I've ever made for my faith. I do believe that God is love, *complete love*, and that his love becomes infinitely bigger and better when you stretch it from a newborn infant all the way to a universal scale. Plus, with string theory, there may be multi universal layers separated by patterns in dark matter vibration sequences . . . sorry, my bad. In other words, God is larger than measurement, and that means his love is also very, *very* big. Then there's the opposite too. If God is love, then that also makes love personal and more understandable . . . even

14

on the smallest, tiny little blue planet speck of dust, human, personal, you level.

MATH AND LOVE

Chad,

I'm a pretty normal male teenager, I'd say. But somehow or another, I keep messing up relationships. Don't get me wrong, I've never really dated. But the reason for that is mostly because whenever I like a girl, she doesn't like me. I have a group of close friends, and I'm the only one in the group who hasn't been involved romantically whatsoever with anyone. Actually, I know a lot of people who have dated, and they're only around fifteen or sixteen. I feel alone and left out, like no matter what I do, I'll just keep getting shot down.

—Confused and Worried

Let's talk to all the "Confused and Worried" out there for a moment. It will help if we add some math to this love confusion. Start with some simple facts. In 2011, 134 million people were born. The United Nations estimates that there are just over 7 billion people alive today. That's 7 billion people sharing the trees, oceans, stop signs, food, and boy band music, which is less important than the other things.

The next bit of information will also not make you feel any better about love. Sorry. But then keep reading . . .

99 PERCENT REJECTION IS AMAZING

What's the point of those people numbers? It's to put rejection in perspective. Sometimes the way we all think about rejection is just stupid. And even the math says so. For example . . . let's say that you are a girl, and you go on 100 dates with 100 different guys. Of those dates, 99 don't go well, at all (and many go horribly). How do you feel about this?

☐ really, really good
☐ super really not good . . . a lot

If you said "super really not good," then I have some bad news: you are terrible at math, and you are missing an important point about how many people might like you. So I'll explain.

If I told you that 99 percent of guys out there won't like you romantically and that only 1 percent of them would, you might start to feel a little depressed. Who loves a 99 percent rejection rate? But here's the thing: if only 1 percent of guys on this planet like you—*only 1 percent*—know what that means? To help you, it means roughly 35 million people of the opposite sex *will* be very interested in you, and that's with a 99 percent fail rate! And you know that more than 1 out of 100 people would like you on average, right? Let's say maybe you also smell really bad, so only 3 or 4 out of 100 like you. But you know what that means, Stinky? Over 100 million people would be interested in you! Who would get sad knowing that, on average, about 35 to 100 million people on this planet would be interested in them romantically, if they could only find the time to meet more people? Do you get this point at all? How we see things changes the things we see.

But how dumb are we sometimes? I mean that seriously too, because how many times do we focus on the rejection part of life? It's like we ignore all of the other acceptance and love in the world to spend time feeling the rejection of one person. That sounds pretty silly, especially considering tens of millions of people could like you, mathematically speaking.

Love Is Not Paradise

Two things are necessary for life: loving and being loved. But romantic love is different. Contrary to popular everything all the time, romantic love is *not* the "end all and be all" of life. Nor is it the only thing that will keep our hearts beating and smiling. There are lots of kinds of love: love of family, love of friends, and, yes, even self-love (in the non-perverted, healthy, balanced sort of way, of course). Romantic love can be wonderful, deep, and fulfilling, but here is what it's not: love is not paradise, nor is it meant to be. Romantic love should complement a well-rounded, meaningful life. It's not meant to *be* your whole life. People who act as though being in love *is* life usually also love listening to their heart and feelings. And if you're one of those people who's only listening to their heart and feelings, then maybe we should look at what you're really doing.

Follow Your Heart . . . to Be Miserable

> *Follow, follow, follow. Just follow, baby, follow.*
> *You just follow that heart . . . girl . . . yada yada.*

Maybe these will be lyrics somewhere in a hit pop song soon, but here's why I don't like them, and I hope you won't either. Everyone tells you to follow your heart. *If you aren't truly listening to that heart of yours*, they say, *then you don't have a big heart.* These people also say sappy things like:

> Follow your heart regardless of what others tell you to do.
> Break the rules and stand apart: ignore your head and
>   follow your heart.
> Have the courage to follow your heart, and you'll know
>   who you truly want to become.

The problem with that whole heart-following thing is that the people who love these sappy sayings the most should probably be listening to them the least. I'm sure that they're kind, good-hearted people, and good for them. But half the time they don't even know what these sayings mean. I know this because I ask people sometimes, and then it gets awkward when they realize *I know* they don't know, and that's why I was asking. My point is that people who throw these sayings around can unintentionally give themselves and other people absolutely horrible advice.

Just to be completely unromantic about it, I want to translate what "Always follow your heart," "Listen to your heart," or "Trust your heart" really means. For starters, let's look at it sarcastically; it's more fun.

So . . . the heart can't lead anything. It has to stay inside of your chest and pump blood to your body, mostly because it's just an organ in your body. In other words, if your heart is leading you, it's outside your body, and you're most likely dead. Also, that thing has absolutely no navigational skills, no GPS, and no wilderness mapping training. The heart also has no mouth (almost positive)—so it can't say anything for you to listen to. So what these kinds of sayings really mean is "trust in your pulmonary system," and that's really dumb advice for relationships.

{

While the world says to follow your heart, the Bible says you should lead your heart.

—chad

He who trusts in his own heart is a fool.
—Proverbs 28:26 NKJV

}

So what about all the "listen to your heart and follow it wherever it takes you" answers? Well, not every answer is a good answer. Are there other suggestions out there? Turns out there are. The Bible often says exactly the opposite of all the cutesy-heart-face-quotey-life-pics, even though I didn't know that for a long time. While the world says to follow your heart, the Bible says you should lead your heart. (And keep in mind, "heart" really means "emotions.") Here are a few quotes:

- The heart is deceitful above all things. (Jeremiah 17:9)
- Be transformed by the renewing of your mind. (Romans 12:2)
- Trust in the LORD with all your heart. (Proverbs 3:5)

Not only does the Bible often say the opposite of the "follow your heart" cutesy sayings club, but it also talks about the consequences for people who actually do follow their hearts:

> There is a way that seems right to a man, but in the end it leads to death.
> —Proverbs 14:12

The writer in Proverbs was actually talking about the danger of following your heart. Coincidentally, this perspective about being led by emotions and emotional confusion is right on par with Therapy 101. Actually, the Bible has a lot of common-sense advice, and I like that a lot. In case you didn't know a little factoid, I like this one: the Ten Commandments—do not steal, murder, and so forth—all speak to the need for controlling our feelings and emotions so that they don't control us. It's the same message a good therapist would give you, just worded a little differently: recognize your feelings, use your brain, and *then* act accordingly.

To put it simply, we could benefit from "un-following" our hearts sometimes and trying to use our brains more—which we are supposed to be developing in very important ways right now anyway. It's kind of like walking a dog. Things work out better for everyone when you lead the dog instead of it leading you. If you are devoted to the teachings of the Dog Training Emperor of the World, Cesar Millan, then you understand this.

So maybe both the Dog Whisperer and the Bible are packed with incredible life lessons. Thank you, Jesus Christ and Cesar Millan, in that order.

THE TRUTH OF THE MAGNET MATTER

Chad,

Hi, I have a kind of broad question. Why does love have to be so difficult? Why can't it be easier?

—Emilia

Honestly, that's a really simple but good question that Emilia asks. To understand it, we have to start somewhere else—at the beginning. That is, why are we attracted to the people we are attracted to? 'Cause it's not always for the reasons we think.

Here's the truth about why we are drawn to certain people, often without knowing it: If you are sad, you tend to attract sad people. If you are lonely, you tend to attract lonely people. And the weird part is that we usually have *no* idea that we're doing this, and yet these unconscious decisions shape a lot of our choices and directions in life. It means a lot of the hurt or rejection or silly relationships that you showed interest in last week, last month, or in your whole life . . . are really a reflection of you. It's not a coincidence that we are drawn to certain types of people or that we repeat the same patterns in relationships. It's not always easy to see this, but it happens a lot. I mean, there's a reason we have sayings like . . .

21

> It was over before it began.
>
> Their love was doomed.
>
> I saw that one coming.
>
> They just weren't right for each other.
>
> Like two doomed ships that pass in a storm.
>
> They never stood a chance.

Why can't love be easier? Well, I don't know. That's a complicated question without one simple answer. I think love can be easy, but it's also a very complex thing too. Maybe instead of finding yourself heartbroken and then asking, "Why is love so difficult?" you should start more simply. Maybe with . . . "What is love?"

Sooo, What Is Love?

How do people know if they're really in love and not just in infatuation? How does a couple know when they should get married and spend the rest of their lives together?

To be honest, I hope the question "Is this really love?" isn't one that you have to struggle with too often or too early. The reason I hope this is because it's a distraction for a lot of people, in very serious ways. There are real things that you need to learn and develop as a young person, and in your teen years, figuring out who you are and where you're headed is key. Inevitably, however, love will draw you in; you can't avoid it and shouldn't. But as you learn and grow and start to look for love, it's important to know what love is . . . and what it is not. To throw out just

22

a few, here are some of the characteristics of actual relationships that are loving:

1. A loving relationship requires two people who feel the same way—or very, very similar—about each other. Just because "you are in love" doesn't mean "we are in love."

2. A loving relationship requires mutual feelings of care and concern, but it also commits to acting in a way that shows that care and concern.

3. A loving relationship requires availability, time, investment, and energy—from *both* of you. Love is not one person trying to make a relationship work. That's unbalanced.

4. People in loving relationships experience joy, peace, comfort, and lower stress levels. If a relationship frequently causes stress and strain, then it probably isn't a loving relationship.

5. People in loving relationships usually have common interests, goals, morals, and faith viewpoints. These similarities draw them closer as they experience more things together naturally through their interests. Opposites may attract, but if one person only likes to ride bikes and the other person only likes to scuba dive, they'll be living in two different worlds.

6. A real loving relationship helps people feel better about life and who they are in life. It gives them a sense of inner peace, not confusion and frustration. Real love says, "I love you, and I know how much you love me."[5]

What I hope you discover about love is this: real love is very reasonable. Deep, romantic, kind, long-lasting, cherished love is very . . . reasonable. And you know what? That's not un-romantic either; it just means more people are capable of it.

By the way, the whole "love as a reasonable and respect-able relationship" thing doesn't sell well—just think about all of the dysfunctional reality shows that play off of love drama. A lack of seeing real love represented in the popular culture we consume adds to our confusion about it. Personally, I don't think love is supposed to be the crazy-dramatic roller coaster ride of life. That's what roller coasters are for. Love . . . is much better than that.

chapter

WE SHOULD BREAK UP
FOR SURE . . . MAYBE

{
Let us not look back in anger,
nor forward in fear, but around in
awareness.

—James Thurber
}

I'M BREAKING UP WITH YOU

We need to break up. It's you, it's me, and it's definitely you and me. It's the *we* that's really the problem. Things obviously haven't been blissful between us, as you might have noticed. We've been arguing more, and I have different things I want to do with my time, as do you. The longer we are in this relationship, the less optimistic about love it makes both of us.

You're frustrated because I'm not meeting your expectations, and I'm frustrated that your expectations are different from mine. I find that I would rather not date anyone than be in a relationship with you at this time. So I think it's time we end this romantic experience. I believe this is the best decision for me, and ultimately it will be the best decision for you as well. And by the end of this chapter, I have hope that you'll understand what I mean by these words. Best wishes to you, and I look forward to valuing everything about you . . . minus all the romantic stuff.

—chad

People hate breaking up for lots of good reasons: it's super un-fun, people don't usually take it well, it's awkward and uncomfortable, emotions get intense, tears are awful, and lots of other reasons that don't need listing. Personally, I'd prefer to sort through garbage or get punched in the face than tell someone I want to break up with them, even if I need to. I mean, maybe some people enjoy sorting garbage or getting punched, but not this guy, and maybe not you either.

So we can all agree that breakups are at the top of the not-fun and not-awesome list of things to do in life, ever. But when it's necessary to end a relationship, how do you do it? What do you avoid? How do you know if you really should break up in the first place? Well . . . let's start with the last one and go from there.

IT'S REALLY ABOUT YOU

How do you know if you should end it or not? Well . . . that's a simple question with quite a few answers. First, why are you dating? I mean, no, for real, why? Do you know? Not just "because I want to" or minimal English word explanations like that. I mean . . . why do you do the things you do, like date? Why do you—and people in general—date the way you do? After all, whether or not you date is really your decision. It's not something you should do just because your friends are doing it. So have you ever made a list of reasons why you are dating, or want to be dating, someone in the first place? A great thing to do for your mind is to put your thoughts on paper; this makes them visually more real. So jot down a few of the reasons you are in, or want to be in, a relationship.

Why I'm in—or want to be in—a relationship . . .

_____

_____

_____

_____

_____

_____

After all, if you don't know why you *choose* to be in a relationship, then you won't know why you should *un-choose* to be in a relationship. And this is really important.

BREAKUPS ARE PROOF WE'RE ALL NUTS

Here are a few important facts:

- The earth spins at 1,040 mph if you live near the equator.[1]
- Dolphins live underwater and are neat.
- Guys look at girls a lot.
- People break up.

Three of these are facts that people accept without argument. But then . . . for some odd reason, people reject the last one. Our brains can seem to turn off when it comes to dating. For example:

Girl starts dating guy. Girl likes guy, girl sees guy's good qualities, and girl enjoys his company and cuteness.

That's lovely and sweet, and I mean . . . yay, but then the crazy turns on. For some reason that escapes me, we forget to even consider that it might not last forever. And that is pretty weird. After all, you're choosing one person from roughly 7 billion or so to be your significant other. There's a chance that you might not get it right the first time, or the second. I mean . . . seriously, there are a lot of variables for why relationships end. One or both of you might have a change of mind or a change of heart. Maybe it's not the right time for you or him. Maybe he moves, gets a job, or picks up a sport that takes up too much of his time, or maybe he decides to live in a tree and only talk to puppets and people on Skype. Or maybe, just maybe, dating someone makes you realize that you do not, in fact, want to date that person. Relationships

begin and relation-
ships end. It's not fun
when they end, but
it happens often and
in most cases . . . for
pretty good reasons.

> If you start dating a particular someone, there are decent odds that you might also have to stop dating this particular someone.

So just remember this: if you start dating a particular someone, there are decent odds that you might also have to stop dating this particular someone.

So Why Break Up?

First, the basic question, "Why?" Why should you break up with someone? Are there right or wrong reasons for breaking up? And if so, what are they and why? In my experience with people, too many don't seem to know what qualifies as a "good reason" to break up with someone. Consider the reasons listed here. Which of them might you think are "good enough" reasons to stop dating someone? Would a good reason be because he or she . . .

- smells bad.
- won't listen to you.
- cares too much about the needs of other people.
- disrespects you in front of other people.
- likes animals too much.
- cheated on you.
- won't talk to you.
- is really tall.

29

- has moral values or physical habits that you disagree with (sexual habits, religious differences, drinking . . . the list goes on . . . and on).
- likes different music than you do.
- has a personality that's *reallly* different from yours.
- has a personality that's *juuust* like yours.

Question for you: As you read through this list . . . did you find yourself saying yes or no to certain statements? Most people do—that's why I ask. But here's the tricky thing—any of these reasons could be right reasons. I mean, obviously some of them are easier to agree with than others. Breaking up with someone who is really tall, for example, might seem shallow. But it could actually have to do with physical attraction, genetics, height differences, and the fact that some people are more affected by physical attraction than others. Having different tastes in music may seem like a petty reason to break up with someone, but different styles in music are associated with different styles in clothing, attitudes, hobbies, types of friends, and so on. Most people get along better with people of similar personalities, while some (not that many) do better with opposite personalities.

The reality of things is this: you get to choose the reasons you like or don't like people. It's that simple. Of course, the flip side is that other people get to choose too . . . so behave, or whatever.

IT'S NOT WRONG TO CHANGE YOUR MIND

I change my mind constantly, and I'm guessing you do too. It's called "changing your mind" for a reason, after all. So what if the decision to break up isn't because of something bad? What if you are simply seeing things more clearly?

Chad,

I don't know if I should break up with my boyfriend. I keep think-ing that I want to, but I find myself not being able to end it, and I'm confused. We are very different, to say the least. I like him, he is nice to me, and we have a "good relationship," as most people say. The reasons I don't want to be with him anymore make me feel bad. We have very different friends, and I also don't think I want to spend as much time with a guy right now as I thought I did. I think I like him as a friend, and only a friend, but I don't know how to tell him that without it killing him, and he didn't do any-thing bad or mean. Help me, because I don't know what to do. He's not doing anything wrong, so is it really okay to end a relationship for no real reason?

—Kelsey

Situations like Kelsey's are difficult because there isn't a big problem. Not having a big reason to break up is kinda . . . weird. It's not like he's lying or cheating or bullying her. So why end a relationship if there isn't a "real problem"? Well, for starters, the "problem" has more to do with Kelsey. And it isn't even a problem—it's actually a good thing and more of a sign that she is growing up. Kelsey has realized that the romance isn't gonna work with soon-to-be-sad boy. She has most likely confused friendship with something more. It happens. And just so you know . . . Kelsey's feelings are completely valid. She just doesn't believe they are, at least not yet.

> { Kindness is the language which the deaf can hear and the blind can see.
> —Mark Twain }

Dating, in essence, is the time when you start to figure out what qualities you are looking for in a future spouse. Just as importantly . . . it's also the time when you figure out what you are not looking for. In dating relationships, you are allowed to decide that someone isn't right for you romantically without feeling terrible about it. I don't know why that feels so strange sometimes, but it is, in fact, true. Be kind, be considerate, but don't let guilt make you keep dating someone who is wrong for you. It's okay to simply change your mind about who you date.

If I had never changed my mind about what I wanted in a relationship or about what I wanted out of a relationship, do you know who I'd be with? Probably not, but I do:

SUSAN: former crush from the third grade

ATTRIBUTES: blonde hair, proficient at reading and writing, great at freeze tag, excellent at all recess and playground activities

RELATIONSHIP STRENGTHS: female, talked to me, shared her fruit snacks with me, didn't hate me

RELATIONSHIP PITFALLS: I like things other than recess now; the qualities I liked in third grade might not be enough for a healthy adult relationship . . . but having fruit snacks never hurts

In other words, my expectations, likes, dislikes, and views about people have changed since third grade, and they continue to change—just as yours will. And you know what? That's a good thing. You absolutely need to reevaluate yourself, other people, and your relationships, and then make changes wherever you need to. And in the dating world, that can mean breaking up. Not everyone who shares his gummy worms with you needs to be your soul mate. You change, I change, we all change; it's just a part of life. Good thing fruit snacks mostly stay the same.

Breakfast and Breakups

You eat because you need to, and usually several times a day. But when you sit down with a bowl of cereal, are you filled with fear? I'm guessing not, unless you've had a tragic encounter with cereal in your life. (If this is true, I'm sorry, because cereal is delicious.) So when you eat a bowl of cereal, do you experience anxiety or anger? Do you try to avoid it? Probably not. Even if you don't love cereal, you probably aren't afraid of it. Why? The reason for this silly example is simple: breakfast is just part of life—it keeps you healthy, and you're used to it. Sometimes . . . cereal just happens.

And sometimes breakups happen; they're part of life. While you may not enjoy breaking up, it's something you need to do. Probably no one has ever said, "I break up with people like I'm eating breakfast." (That's weird.) But sometimes life is just about doing the healthy thing, and breakfast and breakups can fall into that category. Also breathing.

❈ ❈ ❈

Breakups can happen simply because you change your mind or because things just aren't working out. Nothing is particularly wrong; it's just not particularly right either. And that's okay.

But sometimes . . . things really are wrong, and there are good reasons to break up. You know, the warning signs and red flags in relationships. You will want to learn more about this red flag system for your future. I'd say it's pretty critical stuff.

NICE TO MEET YOU— I'M A RED FLAG

{ red flag: a warning signal
—*Merriam-Webster*[1] }

Red is the color of many significant things, and one of them is the red warning sign. For example, we all know a red light means stop your car super soon or you'll crash into something. A red flag at the beach means, "Stop! It's dangerous to swim here." And a relationship red flag means, "Stop! Pay attention! This is important!" Relationship red flags usually mean it's time either to change things or to end things soon. Let's meet some of these red flags.

The Red Flags

Happiness Levels Tanking

Sometimes red flags are simple. If you aren't happier *in* a relationship than you were *out* of it, that's a strong sign you need to change things.

How many people in your life add more stress, drama, and frustration to their lives because of the relationships they have? I mean . . . I can name dozens. It's disheartening to me when I think about normal dating relationships today, because dating isn't meant to teach us about fighting or conflict or compromise. Those lessons are the byproducts of relationships, not the reason for them.

Dating really is meant to be a good thing. It's not always easy or simple, but it should make you happier and more optimistic about human beings in general. I mean . . . that's not asking a lot. My own personal motto-rule-type thingy (or whatever you call it) is 90/10. Dating should be really fun and easy about 90 percent of the time, maybe more. I hope you believe me: dating is the gym class of life, not the advanced calculus class. If dating a person is really difficult, then don't date that person. Maybe even take a total break from dating. It's not the end of the world if you take a time-out. Dating should involve lots of laughing and happy faces, not be filled with brokenness and heartache and cynicism.

Figure out who you are, what makes you happy, and what kind of person you want to date. It's better to be single and happy with who you are than to be miserable in a dating relationship. I swear to you, this is true. There's also no downside to taking a break from dating . . . unless you're involved in a dating competition, and if so . . . *eww*.

MORAL COMPROMISES

People who have different morals, values, and beliefs in their lives will clash. It's just a basic fact. The thing is, your morals, values, and beliefs are the very backbone of your identity. They are what make you who you are. And in your teen years, they are also still being formed. If someone close to you has morals that conflict with yours, then you are in danger of compromising your morals. So . . . don't do that. Here's a pretty good illustration of that: if you are standing up on a chair, it's easier to get pulled off that chair than it is to pull someone up there with you. It's the same way with your morals—there's no upside to compromise. Plus, getting pulled off chairs really hurts. I broke my wrist that way in the sixth grade, pulled off an orange kiddie chair by a girl stronger than me, apparently. I'm telling you, in all seriousness, chairs are out to kill you. Try to stay away from killer chairs . . . and moral compromises.

FAITH DIFFERENCES

Faith isn't something that people just believe in; it's something they live out in their lives. It's the lens through which we see all things, and it's important. It always has been and always will be. For me, having friends of different perspectives and different faiths is really valuable to me; it challenges and strengthens my own faith. But when it comes to romance and relationships, having a different faith perspective than the person you're dating, well . . . it gets tricky.

Every major religion speaks about the importance of "looking through the same lens of faith" as those people who are closest to you. Boyfriends and girlfriends are important relationships and, therefore, are no exception. For Christians, it is and should be a hugely important thing. In 2 Corinthians, Paul writes to this new church formed in Corinth about this issue in particular. He says something very bold sounding when he writes that they shouldn't "be yoked together with unbelievers" (6:14). It wasn't mean; it was meant to protect.

Faith is integrated into everything we do, whether we like it or not. It's not just a categorical box next to "city of birth" on a profile. It helps describe who we are, where we came from, where we are going, and how we live our lives, on a personal level as well as a historical one. It would be weird to think that faith doesn't have much to do with relationships. How can it not? I say this on a personal level, because it's important for me to know that the people closest to me in life are able to understand my joys, fears, hopes, and questions with a similar outlook, which includes my faith in a vital way. It's not just faith either, because things like morality, ethics, and values specifically overlap with faith. If you and the person you're dating aren't viewing the world with the same basic sets of beliefs, then you're going to be seeing the world differently all together. And that's a red flag.

YOU RATIONALIZE BAD THINGS

Have you found yourself saying things like . . .

- I probably expect too much.
- It's better than being alone.
- Yeah, it's not great, but I really do love him.
- It will hurt her if I just end it.
- I just misunderstood what he was really trying to say (or do).
- It will get better if I just keep trying. I just need to be patient.

If you are saying things like these, that would be a red flag. People mistakenly use really great traits, like love and patience and understanding, to justify staying in bad relationships. But statements like these are very clearly *rationalizing*, and they are just not true. Rationalizing bad behavior, especially using virtuous qualities, is a sneaky but damaging habit and can lead to a host of problems, and you don't want a host of anything . . . usually. For starters, you leave yourself open to being used and walked all over, and you become a magnet for unhealthy people, and that . . . is crazy.

By the way, do you really know why a "crazy person" is usually considered crazy, clinically speaking? The basic definition of *crazy* is when a person cannot tell or accept the difference between the way things really *are* in the world and the way he or she *wants* things to be in the world. For people who exhibit "crazy" behavior, or a bunch of obvious emotional issues, or have psychological disabilities, their reality is often not everyone else's reality. This helps to explain things like schizophrenia, for example. But this craziness can show up in relationships too. We do the same thing that makes other people unstable: we look at the world we want to see instead of the world we are standing in. We aren't looking at reality, that's plain but *not* simple. To have healthy relationships, you have to face reality—even if reality ends the relationship.

The easiest way to avoid crazy is to decide what you expect out of a dating relationship—and stick to it. You have to have some sort of expectations, or you'll hate life and dating, so you might as well make them good expectations. It's the best way to attract the emotionally healthy people you want to date while helping to repel the other *"No, thank you, but best of luck to you"* individuals.

AGE

This is kind of simple and overlooked, but when you are thirty, two or three or five years difference in your ages doesn't really matter. But in high school, age differences are magnified—greatly. They make a huge difference, and just a couple of years can be a big enough factor to cause a relationship not to work. Timing really is important, including the times and dates of your birth.

Age difference is also a significant sign of danger. The older people are, the more easily you are influenced by them. For example, the teenage girl who gets pregnant is, on average, six years younger than the male who gets her pregnant. That's tragic, also unfortunate, and often illegal. More importantly, it's also unnecessary. The biggest risk factor in teen pregnancy, in fact, might be age difference by itself. It means that the guy can more easily control and influence the girl. If the girl were older, she would have seen that guy's kind of behavior before, been better able to recognize it for what it really was, and been more likely to say no. Biologically speaking, each year of your adolescence has very different life experiences attached to it. Older people often have the upper hand in relationships because they know more and therefore have more experience by default. This makes things unequal, and relationships should always have equality at their center.

And yes, the age people start dating is significant—how could it not be? If you're twelve, be twelve, not twenty. You'll regret being twenty when you're twelve, I promise absolutely. I'm not telling you what to do, but I am telling you with personal certainty and lots of facts . . . there isn't any upside to dating before you're sixteen. There is, however, an upside to waiting to date. Your odds of having better relationships get better the older you are. The evidence on this is overwhelmingly clear: teens who date later rather than sooner are happier, better prepared for the complexities of romantic relationships, and have a better sense of who they are as an individual.

I actually never really dated anyone until the beginning of college, and I don't regret it at all. My relationship-crazed friends weren't any happier than I was, but they did seem more stressed. They didn't usually seem to have as much fun either. There's no benefit in trying to grow up too fast. You'll get wrinkles soon enough; don't rush them.[2]

BAD COMMUNICATION

Chad,

I've been dating this guy for a few weeks now. I feel like he doesn't want to talk to me, give me a hug, or even hold my hand. I never know what he's thinking, and I don't know what to do!

—Riley

Humans have the exceptionally unique ability to use words to express themselves . . . and it's super-duper, extra vitally, necessarily important. Considering how much we talk, having bad communication skills makes it virtually impossible to have a good relationship. If you find yourself relating to any of Riley's thoughts, then . . . hi, here's a red flag!

It takes a basic level of communication skills, especially verbal communication skills, to have a real functioning relationship outside of the playground. Communication is like oxygen to a relationship. If someone doesn't have these skills, or doesn't use them by talking to you and listening to you, then that's a problem. Often a lack of communication just means that the person is too young and hasn't developed the skills to have a good dating relationship yet. It may also be a red flag for some other issues. Either way, it takes quite some time to develop communication skills, and these are things that you *cannot* change for someone—you just can't. Wait; is that an exit sign over there?

ATTRACTION

Ummm . . . physical attraction is important. The sun is also hot. I find it funny and then sad, in that order, that we still seem ashamed of physical attraction. I mean, it's not the only thing that's important, for sure, but it is still *a thing*. And attraction isn't limited to strikingly handsome or exotic features, just in case you were being shallow. It's a combination of many things, including biology, height, weight, physical features, skin color, pheromones, basic personality types (there are many), voice tone and pitch, and social interaction, personally and in a group setting. Physical attraction *is* a significant thing—and if you make sure not to give it too much significance, then we'll be fine. People are cute, and we like to look at each other. Get over it, vision haters.

Our culture shines a giant LED spotlight on physical attractiveness. So it's practically impossible to avoid being influenced by these attitudes. It's like finding yourself shipwrecked in the Pacific and swimming in saltwater—eventually you will swallow some of it, even if it makes you sick. In the same way, the obsession with a small, shallow, and stupid view of what it means to be attractive is also something that will make you sick. People are more than hot, funny, cute, quiet, dumb, sexy, sweet, smart, or weird. We really should extend our vocabulary of the human spirit, after all. And just because you're physically attracted to someone doesn't mean you have to date them either. I know a lot of guys who might date a girl because she is hot, and almost completely forget whether or not they liked her as a person first. Guys are extra dumb like that sometimes, but so are gals. We all act dumb like this sometimes. Point is . . . make sure there is more to your relationship than hormones, as fun as hormones may be.

CHILDISHNESS

Just because someone is in a relationship doesn't mean that person is mature enough to be in a relationship. Four-year-olds could say they're dating and really believe it, but they'd still be four, wouldn't they? Childish behavior and immaturity aren't your problem—unless you're childish and immature, then, yes, they're your problem. But if they aren't your problem, don't make them yours. Whether it's too much video game time, talking in little kid voices, teasing and taunting, being physically aggressive, being loud at odd or inappropriate times, causing arguments, or any other "childish" behaviors—it doesn't matter. I'm pretty sure you don't want to date a child. That's commonly referred to as "all kinds of messed up" in street language.

There's one more important question for the person who is dating someone childish. That is . . . *why are YOU drawn to someone who is being so childish?* And the answer of "I didn't know he was really like that until we dated" is not good enough. Unless you started dating the very second you met a person, then that's probably not true. So . . . why did you ignore the stuff you knew? Sometimes it's that people can't distinguish between healthy and unhealthy behaviors; other times it's because people like the idea of playing the parent. Sounds gross maybe, but it happens, *a lot*. People who are drawn to immature behavior either relate to it, or they want to be the "parent" who helps change it. So if you see childishness as a problem in your relationship, the red flag might really be about you. It's okay, we all have flags at some point. But when we see them, we need to stop and pay attention. Flags are there to tell us something important—like it's time to make a change.

DISTANCE

Some people seem to do okay with long-distance relationships. For others—the majority, it seems—it's too big a hurdle to overcome at the end of the day. Distance tends to create struggles and conflicts that wouldn't exist otherwise; time being the big one. It's a lot harder to spend time getting to know each other if you aren't in the same physical space and zip code.

Personally, it would be too hard for me to have a relationship with someone I can't be in the same place with. If we can't look directly at each other, hold hands, eat food together, and make all those little unspoken gestures that can't be done on the phone or Skype or by text, then it just doesn't work for me. Communication, after all, is at the heart of any relationship, and it has a lot to do with the unspoken things in life, like body language, eye contact, touch, and all those little meanings we only pick up in person. For me, that is vital, and so is being in the same zip code eventually.

Distance carries other obstacles to a good relationship, like having different friends, social ties, hangouts, and hobbies. It also takes a lot more energy and effort to maintain a long-distance relationship. And you may find that it's more effort than it's worth. That might sound unromantic, but it's pretty impossible to be romantic when you're exhausted.

VICTIMS AND DRAMA LOVERS

{ dra-mat-ic: of or relating to the
drama
—*Merriam-Webster*[3]

dramatians: they hate it but create it
—chad }

We'll talk about this more in depth in chapter 7, "Why It Hurts." But just know that if the person you're dating is stuck in a victim role or seems to be a magnet for drama, then seriously, no. Just don't. It will stress you out, so if you're smart, just don't. These kinds of habits aren't changed overnight, and it's not in your best interest to stick around and take on other people's issues, because then they'll become your issues. You don't need more issues; you need fewer issues.

If, on the other hand, *you* are the one with the issues—and it happens—then spend some time on your own and deal with your issues. It's not easy to do, but it's the best answer for all of us. Spend time learning to be a healthier individual. I'm not a mathematician, but I'm thinking a lot more healthier individuals probably team up to be healthier couples, just saying.

LOSING YOURSELF

Chad,

So here's my problem. I've never been guy crazy. I've only had one boyfriend, and it's not been going that great. Not terrible,

46

but not great. Here's the thing, though: I find myself constantly freaking out over things with him. I've noticed the last couple months, and my friends have too, how much I seem to cling to him, and I feel like I'm losing my personality. I don't want a guy to have to be the one to make me feel special (I have great parents and love God), but I can't help feeling like my feelings about him get more and more out of control, and it's really confusing. I don't know if it's me or him or something I just don't get. I would appreciate any advice about this.

—Ashtin

Do you feel a strong urge to change, adapt, or blend in with a particular group? Do you find yourself keeping your ideas, thoughts, and opinions to yourself so that you won't upset your datey-person? Do you go along with what your date does or says or believes just to keep things happy? These are red flags—a warning about losing your own identity.

Dating shouldn't suppress who you are; it should help you grow as a person. Because you only have a certain number of years to develop your unique self and to develop into an adult, this becomes crucial. Finding your identity is obviously kind of important, but it's somewhat optional . . . which is scary. Repressing your own identity just to make someone like you is one of the most incredibly harmful things that you can do in life. It's not just a red flag. It's a flashing, neon-red billboard with a red flag of a red flag on it. Tip for life: always pay attention to flashing red billboards in your life.

CONTROLLING PEOPLE

This red flag has several dangerous elements to it. Controlling people act out of fear, and they inevitably cause harm.

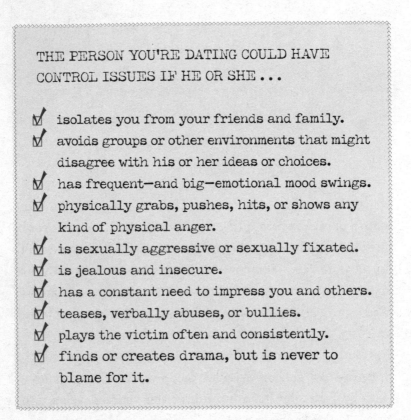

THE PERSON YOU'RE DATING COULD HAVE
CONTROL ISSUES IF HE OR SHE . . .

☑ isolates you from your friends and family.
☑ avoids groups or other environments that might disagree with his or her ideas or choices.
☑ has frequent—and big—emotional mood swings.
☑ physically grabs, pushes, hits, or shows any kind of physical anger.
☑ is sexually aggressive or sexually fixated.
☑ is jealous and insecure.
☑ has a constant need to impress you and others.
☑ teases, verbally abuses, or bullies.
☑ plays the victim often and consistently.
☑ finds or creates drama, but is never to blame for it.

Dating a controlling person—or being one—is dangerous in three ways: First, you are affected by these unhealthy behaviors, whether you want to be or not. Second, it could mean that controlling behavior is appealing to you. And third, you are more likely to find these things again in the next person you date.

Adults who are controlling in their relationships—as well

as those who let themselves be controlled—almost always began those habits in younger relationships. Your life doesn't start later. It's decided by the little choices you make right now. Some try to "love that person into love," but that doesn't really work. So if your significant other, or "sother," shows signs of being controlling, it's best to say bye early. And if you're the one who is controlling, look in the mirror for a while, 'cause you don't want to be someone else's red flag either.[4]

INSECURITY, JEALOUSY, SELFISHNESS

To make it simple: if the person you're dating is showing signs of insecurity, jealousy, pettiness, selfishness, or just plain weirdness . . . then here is a nice red flag for you. And if *you* are the one showing signs of insecurity, jealousy, pettiness, selfishness, or other weirdness, then . . . ya know, obviously you look good in red to someone. (Just trying to be an optimist about your flag issues.)

Everyone gets insecure, and everyone has their selfish moments, but if it's happening often, then there really is a problem. And okay, so . . . there's a problem. Now what? Well . . . change it then. Talk about why the problem exists and learn about how it needs to change. Then either make those changes or walk away. Love is not insecure, it is not jealous, and it is not selfish. This is part of the famous verse in 1 Corinthians that describes love, and it's still probably the single best description of love in the history of the known world, in case you need something to fall back on when you get confused about what *love really is*. And also these verses can apply directly to any relationship, at any time. 1 Corinthians 13:4–7. Good stuff.

49

{ Better to have loved and lost than to
live with a psycho the rest of your life.
—unknown }

YOUR FRIENDS AND FAMILY SEE WHAT YOU DON'T

Why we disregard other people's opinions about our relationships, especially when they seem concerned, is beyond me, but we sure do it.

The reason others can see things about your relationship that you can't is actually kind of simple: they aren't as emotionally blinded as you are. No, they can't see all the things you can, but they can see behavior without all the emotion attached to it. If you find yourself saying stuff like, "He's not really like that, you just don't know him," then here's your flag. Because odds are when everyone else is screaming, "Yes, he's really like that!" then you're the one not seeing things correctly. If it helps, most people do it at least once. Rookie mistake—just don't repeat it.

ADDICTED TO A PERSON

People are the biggest drug addiction in the world, and I mean that quite literally. Take any single substance abuse problem in the world, and it's dwarfed in comparison to the addiction to feelings and people. This . . . is a very big problem. At best, it's a sign of immaturity, and at worst, it's a sign of mental imbalance.

Beware of people who treat others like a drug they have to have. It can turn into lots of things, one being stalking, which is never, ever good. Stalking is terrible and creepy and embarrassing and dangerous and all kinds of weird things. *Aaaand* now I'm looking behind me. Anyway, addiction and healthy relationships just don't go together. It's like oil and water, or you and a hungry leopard locked together in a small cage. These things don't go together; the proof is on YouTube, people.

AVOIDING PROBLEMS

People avoid unpleasant things, especially conflict in relationships. But part of growing up is learning *not* to avoid things that are difficult or unpleasant. Avoiding has its own consequences, and it can make things even more difficult later on. So not breaking up with someone when you should break up can actually cause more pain now and in the long run for both people.

If you (or the person you are dating) regularly avoid things, act like nothing is wrong, sweep things under the rug, or just act as if problems don't exist, then look at the red flag there. In all reality, you are avoiding reality. So *avoid avoidance.* I'll find a better slogan for that eventually.

YOU'RE A SECRET GENIUS, POTENTIALLY

Just so you know, the red flag thing in this chapter isn't just about dating. These are behaviors that are harmful and unhealthy in any relationship. Learning to recognize these red flags and handle them will greatly affect the quality of your life, the relationships you have, and how well you understand yourself. It doesn't matter if you are the one holding the red flag or if it's your datey-person with the flag. It's about the flag itself and the issue it represents. Red flags don't just go away on their own. You have to change, and that's always the answer anyway. Luckily, you are already a lot smarter and more capable than you give yourself credit for.

You are smarter than you may realize. *Far* smarter, actually. This is why: because you already know these things. I mean it— you already know most of things in this chapter and this book. If you think about this stuff, it's just basic life principles that you've been learning your whole life. For example: Someone who lies is *not* a good friend, so you know that a liar will make an even worse boyfriend or girlfriend. You know that having good friends means being a good friend, so having a good date means being a good date. You also know that there are good ways, and not-so-good ways, to have a relationship with someone. Apply some of the same lessons you know in life to your dating relationship and you have wisdom. To really simplify it, try this . . .

PICTURE SIX-YEAR-OLDS, BUT DON'T BE WEIRD . . .

Picture someone you know. Close your eyes and imagine that person sitting across from you, ranting about a dating problem. Now imagine her as a six-year-old—complete with six-year-old voice and size—saying something like this to her mom:

I don't know what to do, Mommy. He says I'm chubby and dumb, and he makes fun of me around all my friends. But then he told me I'm special and pretty when no one else was around. I'm confused, Mommy, what should I do?

You pretty much know the advice to give that six-year-old, right?

Well, honey, if that boy is mean to you on the slide, you need to ignore him from now on and just go make new friends over on the monkey bars.

We learn this stuff in kindergarten, but somewhere along the way it's like we just forget some of the basics, especially when it comes to dating. Yet the principles are still the same. Respecting yourself and other people is necessary for all relationships. It's the Golden Rule about treating people well and expecting to be treated well in return.

On the playground of life, when someone is rude to you on the slide, it's best to go play on the monkey bars and ignore them. Recess is short, after all.

1　2　3　4

{ Breaking Up }

chapter

BREAKING UP NON-HORRIBLY

> Maybe this breakup will be good for you, since you've never really experienced pain before.

> If the phone doesn't ring, it's probably me.

> It's not me. It's you.

> It's not you; it's me. I'm just totally not interested in you.

HOW TO BREAK UP WITH SOMEONE

Chad,

I think it's time to end my current relationship. It's distracting me. I don't feel the same way that he does, and basically I just need to do it and get it over with, but it's really hard. I was wondering what I can do to prepare for doing this, because I feel awful about it and I know it's going to hurt him. Is there a best way to break up with someone?

—Brooke

Let's be slightly unromantic for a moment. Might as well, it's a chapter about how to break up with someone, so let's get the happy party started. Here's the thing: dating relationships pretty much have one of two possible outcomes—either you will marry the person or you won't. And since most people don't marry the first person they date, then at some point this also means they will break up.

> Most people don't marry the first person they date.

Believe it or not, this chapter about how to break up was actually the easiest chapter to write. Maybe that's helpful to you . . . or maybe not. The thing is this: people are born, people die, people are happy, people are sad, people get together, and . . . people break up. You will most likely have to do it more than once, and you'll probably have it done to you at least once and maybe more. I'm sorry to break the news to you about this—if I did, which I doubt—but you might as well save yourself some stress and heartache by learning from the tens of millions of relationships before yours that . . . well . . . stopped.

Once you've decided to break up with someone (if you're not sure, glance back into the past at chapters 2 and 3), then you just need to know *how* to do it in the most non-horrible way possible. Let's be honest: breaking up or getting broken up with is as fun as falling down stairs in front of people and crying like an infant. Sometimes, though, the worst thing about breaking up is the anticipation of it. Breaking up only takes between two minutes and an hour. At most, it's a conversation, and at the least, it's a declaration and walkaway moment. It's our brains that make it more difficult. When we see breaking up as a really difficult thing, it will be exactly that. I mean, it's already not easy, but it's only worse if we agonize over it or avoid it. Good news: knowing what to do and what to expect will help a lot. There are really only three steps. Not easy, but simple, and at least there are only three. Small victories, right? Yay.

THREE EASY STEPS

Even when you are the one who is ending the relationship, it's hard. But when it has to be done, it's better to just learn to do it well, and do it well once. So here's your how-to in three basic steps:

1. KNOW EXACTLY WHY YOU'RE BREAKING UP

If you've looked at the signs—the red flags—and considered the reasons why you should end the relationship, then it's a good idea to *know* these reasons by heart. Breaking up can be highly emotional, especially when mixed with someone else's emotions. And emotions can wreck your brain's logical plans. That's why you *really* have to know why you are doing what you are about to do.

Think through your reasons for breaking up. You want to be sure of your decisions, after all, and this is an important one. If you aren't sure, this makes you seem uncertain and usually leaves your ex confused. Also, since most people's brains don't do well at remembering things in stressful situations, you have to put a little prep time into this process. In other words, write it out. But—and this is important—this list is for you and no one else. Do *not* take this list and throw it at the person you are breaking up with. Trust me, things will get pretty horrible if you do that. After you know your reasons, then you can find a way to tell the other person in a way that he or she can handle.

It's important to know that less is more when it comes to this subject. Don't defend yourself, just inform the other person simply and honestly. To get you started, consider these reasons:

Pretty Legit Reasons for Making Someone Cry, Be Sad, and All Broked Up

❀ I have changed, and I'm not the same person I was when I started dating you.

❀ I don't feel we communicate well enough.

❋ We argue too much, and it's not good for me anymore.

❋ I don't want to be in a romantic relationship right now. *(Make sure this is a true statement and not just an excuse, or else you're being a mean human being.)*

❋ I've done wrong things. I've lied to you and myself. I've made decisions that have hurt you. I have guilt about this. I need to apologize, but I also need to break up because I'm not ready to be in a relationship right now.

❋ I don't feel ready, or old enough, to be in a relationship.

❋ I'm finding more and more reasons to spend time away from you.

❋ You are controlling and possessive of me, my time, and my life.

❋ There is too much drama in your life.

❋ We have different habits, morals, and/or lifestyles, and they just aren't meshing together well.

❋ I don't have the same intensity of feelings that you do.

❋ We have different expectations of a high school relationship. You expect more than I am able to give right now.

- I am pressured to do things I am not comfortable doing.
- I feel abused (emotionally or physically), and I won't be in a relationship like that.
- I feel smothered.
- We seem to be more like friends than people who are interested in each other romantically.
- I have personal things I need to deal with on my own.
- You are a figment of my imagination. You aren't real, and I have to finally say it out loud. We need to break up with me, and I probably have a counseling appointment I should get to.

Why I Want to Break Up

QUICK, GIANT, WARNING SIGN

Stalking is defined as "virtually any unwanted contact between two people that directly or indirectly communicates a threat or places the victim in fear.'"

Author side note: A lot of people overuse the term *stalker* these days. I hear things like, "Um . . . yeah, stalker dude is creepin' all the time on you." This is usually said by suburban teenagers and their friends to describe an awkward guy who may exhibit some odd behavior around a girl. Usually it's because he's nervous and awkward, but let's be honest . . . that is *not* what a stalker is.

If, however, you feel you *are* actually being stalked, take it very seriously. People do strange things, and it's a real problem. You need to clearly tell that person to leave you alone. Keep in mind: stalkers don't think they're stalkers; it's other people who know they are. (Also . . . if *you're* being weird, ask your friends if you're being kinda stalkerish. Self-check doesn't hurt, ya know?) But if someone else refuses to leave you alone—at any time, not just after a breakup—then calmly and confidently involve parents, principals, or the police. Police exist for a reason. Crimes of passion hurt people every single day, and this is terrible. Be willing to do what a lot of people never do, get help. Pushy and threatening behavior can only exist in the dark, so put a spotlight on it, a high beam, and ask others to do the same. Shine light on dark behavior; it hates being exposed.

2. "THE TALK"

Seriously, and for real, be prepared ahead of time. Know what you are going to say before you have to say it. Keep this in your mind: you are not there to negotiate your relationship; you are there to end it. Explain what you have decided, why you have decided it, and what will happen next. Do all of this quickly but with kindness and respect. Respect—especially when you're about to drop a breaking-up bomb—is crucial. Respect always maintains calmness and dignity. It is the exact opposite of an emotional freak-out, and it works infinitely better.

CHOOSE THE RIGHT SETTING

Setting can be crucial. A lot of people don't consider it, making a hard thing even harder. Breaking up can be highly emotional, so don't do it in front of a bunch of people. You are saying farewell to someone you have cared about and who cares about you, so don't do it over the phone, in the cafeteria, in the hallway, or at one of your "special places" where sentimental memories exist. Choose somewhere neutral, calm, and safe. You might want people nearby, but not too close and not too many. Confusion, crying, and anger—just in case that happens—are not fun to watch. Mostly because you have to pretend that all the other people in Starbucks don't know that your five-dollar chai latte is full of sugar and tears.

DO IT IN PERSON WHENEVER POSSIBLE

It's not fun to look a person in the eye and say, "It's over." But unless it would be dangerous, or they are too far away, it's really important to break up in person. It's a respectful gesture, in the most basic sense of the term. If you have to do it over the phone, or e-mail, or some other way—and I really mean only if you have to—still take time to carefully think out what you want to say. The other person needs to understand what is happening and why so that he or she doesn't end up with emotional or psychological damage. Understanding helps people learn to move on in a healthy way. Put yourself in the other person's shoes: would you rather get dumped and left with a clear explanation or with confusion and uncertainty?

And one more thing: Don't. Just don't. Don't be the texter-breaker-upper. It's stupid, mean, and inconsiderate, and pretty cowardly, whether you're a guy or girl. Golden Rule on this one. Do it in person, kindly, and with some class. Do unto others . . . and all that stuff. Okay, just had to get that out there.

"I" BEFORE "U" EXCEPT WHEN . . . UMM, JUST DON'T SAY "U"

When breaking up with someone, be prepared with simple answers to questions like Why? *Why?* And *WHY?!?* Answer as honestly and simply as possible, focusing on why you are choosing to move on, *not* what is wrong with the other person. I repeat . . . *not what is wrong with the other person.* Whenever a sentence starts with, "You always . . ." or "You never . . . ," the person hearing it will feel your finger of blame being pointed right in his or her face. Don't do that, because it's enraging and makes people hate fingers, and you shouldn't hate fingers, because those things are really important.

It's much better to say, "I haven't felt good about myself in this relationship, and it's best for us not to date anymore," than it is to say, "You just don't seem to care about this relationship." Maybe it sounds wimpy, but the less the blame finger is pointed, the easier it will be. Yes, *you* need to know what you're feeling and why, but you don't necessarily have to share every detail. After all, the goal isn't to get your feelings out; the goal is to end the relationship calmly and quickly. And if you think about it, there's a pretty big difference between the two.

BE HONEST

In the end, we all know honesty is the best policy. So why not start with it? Don't beat around the bush or try to pad things to the point of confusion. The best way to break up with someone is to be honest, direct, and kind. It will be easier in the long run, and he or she will respect you for it . . . eventually. Just not in the same week, probably. I mean, you did just break up.

Don't concern yourself with making sure the other person "takes the news well," because odds are the other person won't. But honesty will help the process—for real it will—and it will help minimize confusion, hurt, and anger for both of you. Who wants more of that stuff anyway? If you do . . . search counselors in your area, 'cause it could be a sign.

MAKE YOUR POINT QUICKLY AND CLEARLY

If you had to fire someone from a job, you wouldn't chat for thirty minutes about nothing and then say, "By the way, you're fired." That would be strange and mean. The same is true with breakups. Tell the person your decision quickly and *calmly*. Do this calmly. You might also want to make sure to do it calmly, and whenever possible, stay calm. Clear on that?

Plan to say less, not more. You can remember a few, well-rehearsed words better than you can many words—and so can the person you're breaking up with. Less, in this case, really is more. Being honest and upfront—and also calm—doesn't give false hope, and it helps you have emotional control over yourself. Speaking of emotions . . .

SLAP YOUR FEELINGS IN THE FACE, BUT JUST FOR A MINUTE

Your emotions need to be the leader in the conversation. Don't let your emotions be dictated by the other person's highly unpredictable emotions, because this happens often. Use the rational functions of your brain at this specific juncture in time, not the emotional ones. So try to deal with your emotions before "the talk"—and then afterward with your best friend, your mom, or someone other than the person you just broke up with. Just don't deal with your emotions during the talk. Also, *not during*. Getting emotional during "the talk" only confuses the other person. It can lead to the other person thinking things like . . . *See, you have doubts about this, or it wouldn't be this hard to do.*

We'll talk more about the five stages of grief and loss and how they relate a little later. But for now, just know that the dumpee will usually go through a very predictable set of feelings and behaviors, including shock and denial. Sometimes people just react. There may be tears, anger, begging, pleading, arguing, or just sitting and staring. One girl told me that she broke up with her boyfriend and the guy just kept burping. So . . . expect the unexpected. Focus on staying calm . . . and avoid burping, when possible, just in case.

SHOULDERS BACK, DARLING

You may not think that body language and composure are important when you break up, but they are actually just as important, maybe more important, than the words you say.

So start with good posture. It sends the message that you are composed and confident. Slouching, on the other hand, shows a lack of confidence and says you're not sure about what you're saying. If you have to, just fake it—probably no one will ever know the difference. Plus, I mean . . . posture is just important, in general. Thank you, breakups, six surgeries, and eighteen months of physical therapy for that overlooked reminder.

No Kidding . . . Be Careful What You Say During the Breakup Talk

Again, people can do strange things . . . just remember that. You may think this person would never do anything strange or hurtful, but anything is possible during a breakup. Be prepared ahead of time, and be careful what you share with people, even if you think your relationship is presently fine. The more personal, vulnerable, or candid things you share, the more material that person has to do strange things with once you do break up. Think rumors, revenge, gossip, half-truths. For crying out loud, just think Internet! In fact, keep the Internet in mind for many of the things you do, actually. I mean . . . you want to avoid the words *personal life* and *Internet* being in the same sentence. So guard your heart . . . and your mouth. Don't say things that could be used against you in the court of breakups.

Please . . . I Beg You . . . Just Don't

There are some things you just really shouldn't do. These are very time tested in the "don't do this" chapter of life. So . . . it's a good list to keep handy:

DON'T . . .

- ☑ KEEP EXPLAINING YOURSELF. Say it once, clearly and calmly. You were heard already.
- ☑ USE FAKE LINES. "It's not you; it's me" may be true, but it's too cliché. It will only make the dumpee feel that you don't care about his or her feelings.
- ☑ BE MEAN. It just makes it worse. Be compassionate. The way you break up with someone says a lot about who you really are.
- ☑ CRY. This is a "Pull yourself together!" moment, people. If your emotions start to take over, take a break or go to the restroom.
- ☑ ARGUE. If you argue or get pulled into an argument, you'll lose. Arguing is a way to keep the conversation going. It can also lead to bringing up past examples, and you don't want to focus on the past.
- ☑ SAY THINGS WHEN YOU ARE HIGHLY EMOTIONAL. You won't say them well, and you might say something that only makes breaking it off harder.
- ☑ ATTEMPT TO CONSOLE YOUR EX. It might seem nice, but it's of no use to that person. You can't break up with *and* comfort a person at the same time. Breaking up is what it is. Being kind and respectful is all you can do.
- ☑ OVERSTAY. Less is more, including time. Say it clearly, and then kindly say, "I think it's best that I go now."

Now . . . Leave

It's not easy to leave when someone isn't happy. But if you know this ahead of time, then it will be a lot easier. Say what you need to say, answer basic questions, and then . . . *leave*. Quickly and calmly.

And FYI, most of the time attempting to leave "on really good terms" just doesn't work. Most breakup conversations simply do not end with hugs and high fives and a milk shake. Maybe someday, in a magical land with unicorns and edible flowers, they will. But for now, say what you need to say, thank the person for listening, and then . . . exit, stage right.

3. What to Expect After the Breakup
Keep Your Distance

Seriously. This is important . . . for both of you. I know it's hard to see someone in pain, especially when you are used to being the one who provides comfort. But when something gets broken, it takes time to heal—it just does. And distance will help both of you heal quicker. You can be kind and cordial, but give a good amount of time for the reality to settle in. This may mean distancing yourself from mutual close friends for a while too. It doesn't have to be permanent, but it's better to create some distance from the things that brought you together.

Choose the High Road . . . Ahead of Time

Before the actual breakup, decide to take the high road, no matter what happens. Make no mistake, what you do after a breakup says more about you than anything else—and it will affect how you feel about yourself later. Make sure you do everything with dignity and respect . . . you'll sleep better.

Lay your head on your pillow at night knowing you have done everything you can to keep your head held high. It might help to remember a few things:

Resist the dumb worldwide announcement.

As tempting as it is, don't go around telling everyone about the breakup. It only prolongs the agony. Tell the people closest to you, but not in a gossipy way. Your goal is to move on, not just vent or relive it. Kids gossip about it; mature young adults talk about it in order to *do* something about it.

The trash talk thing . . .

Trash talk only makes you look bad. People start to think you'll talk about anyone that way. It also puts mutual friends in a difficult spot when you trash talk your ex. You don't want to make friends choose between the two of you. That's insensitive . . . so don't be that.

Don't gossip. None. Zero. Please.

Again, this is about you. People might allow you to gossip, or even expect you to make your ex look bad. Don't. It's just mean and hateful and spiteful . . . and you don't want to be mean or hateful or spiteful. People will not like you, and you won't like your nicknames.

Don't go back and complicate.

Don't call. Don't text. Don't try to keep apologizing. And definitely don't stalk. If you are putting this relationship in the past, then put it there, and leave it there. Stay focused on what's in front of you, not behind.

Don't engage in conflict.

It takes two to fight, so make sure you don't sign up as the second. You can walk away at any time. Sometimes the only way to make the fighting monster go away is to ignore it. No matter how much it growls at you, the only thing it wants is for you to growl back. So don't do that.

The Virtual World of Heartbreak

These days, our identity is pretty connected to the information about us on the Internet. It's a weird time in history, as we mesh our private selves and public selves together, trying to figure out what should be where. For now, err on the side of caution when it comes to posting your personal life and feelings online. Actually, this is a good rule for life, not just for breakups. Seriously, that online stuff never disappears—it's stored, it's saved, it's downloaded, or whatever techni-coded oddness someone comes up with next. The words and pics you post today can come back to bite you years from now in college interviews and job interviews. So be careful with what you reveal about yourself online. It has real implications, and I know a few people who can attest to that fact.

When it comes to breakups, there are some commonsense steps you need to take in the virtual world:

Change your relationship status.

This is kind of a simple thought, but it has its relevance today. Just update your relationship status quietly, or make it nonexistent for a while. Don't draw attention to the situation unnecessarily. It just confuses everyone. Don't splash it all over your Facebook page or tweet it to every person on the planet.

That's immature and self-serving and hurtful. Do it simply and with dignity, or just delete those relationship options off your profiles altogether, and then you won't have to worry about it. It's a basic respect thing.

Purposefully limit your ex's access to you.
It may not be necessary to do this, but sometimes it is. If your ex is not taking the breakup well—as harsh as it may sound—then you need to help him or her close the door. Just limit all access—quietly "unfriend," "unfollow," and "un" whatever else you need to. This applies to the "real world" too—move your seat at lunch and avoid the places where your ex hangs out. Doesn't matter how he reacts; what matters is that you are practicing setting boundaries.

Oh no . . . the pictures?!?
If either of you is having a hard time with the breakup, then removing those pleasant photographic memories from Facebook (or whatever fun pop-up social site comes next) can help signal that it really is over. If you don't want to trash them, download them to a flash drive or your computer. As always, don't be dramatic about it. Just quietly do what needs to be done.

Secuuurittyyy!
Sometimes people get weird after a breakup . . . and it's virtually impossible to tell ahead of time who will get weird and who won't. So if you've shared passwords or other private information, take steps to protect yourself. Change passwords, security codes, and whatever else. I'll say it again:

people can do odd things when jealousy, anger, vengefulness, or sadness hit.

LET FATHER TIME DO HIS THING

After a breakup, you may wonder, *Should I stay in touch or not?* Start by giving it some time—and giving your ex some space. Keeping in touch too much or too soon is usually confusing. This can be difficult, especially if you go to the same school, church, or whatever. Just try to keep your distance, let some time pass, and then reevaluate.

Time helps, it really does, and whether you like it or not, this is a time-tested reality. The intense feelings of a breakup cannot last at that same intensity level forever, especially when they aren't fueled by interactions with that person. Yes, it will be hard for a while, but in the meantime, focus on other things to take up your time. Act respectfully and with class, stick to your good decisions, and it will be clear that you have moved on. People will adjust accordingly; they really will.

If at some point you've *both* moved on emotionally, then sure, be friends. It happens all the time. Just remember, it takes two people who understand this, not one. Until then, if you run into each other, stick with, "I'm doing pretty well, and I hope you are too."

❖ ❖ ❖

Breakups are not fun. Neither are wisdom teeth, cavities, car wrecks, bad breath, and missing socks. It's a simple reality that some things in life aren't pleasant. But the important thing to remember is that behind this breakup "problem," there are people. Real people with real hearts, dreams, fears, and stories. And God loves them just as much as you and me. It's our job to do the best we can in everything, and to try to do it honestly, lovingly, and respectfully. This includes ending a relationship.

At the end of the day, shouldn't we really want the best for everyone? And I mean *everyone*—even those we've broken up with and been hurt or dumped by. So while it's sad when relationships don't work out, it seems like we should still wish the best for everyone, and hope that they would wish us well too. We need a world full of people who are being their best. Plus, it will help with the breakup thing too.

Win-win . . . probably.

HOW TO GET BREAKED UP, BROKENED UP, BROKED UP WITH

{ This just isn't for me. Nothing
personal, I just want to be able to tell
people I'm single.

—unknown }

Sooner or later just about everyone goes through a breakup. Some are worse than others. And sometimes, let's just be honest . . . people are kinda dumb. Dumb is a choice, after all. And sometimes, people who are being really dumb also like to give advice. And sometimes, they are a seventeen-year-old guy writing advice on the best way to dump someone. *And* . . . perhaps a time-out from human activity for a few months would be helpful for them and everyone else.

How to Dump a Girl:

Take her out to a nice Chinese restaurant at least five miles away from her home. Insist that she not bring her purse and that you've got everything covered. Order all kinds of food, pig out, and then tell her that you have to go to the bathroom. When you go, exchange her fortune cookie with one that says, "Ha ha! You're dumped." Leave out the back and stick her with the bill. Then drive away. She'll have no ride, owe a bunch of money, be surrounded by angry restaurant people, and no one will be there to bail her out.

—a teenage boy
(probably unhappy, possibly unstable, and certainly a
bad boyfriend and an overall suspect human being)

Bad breakup stories are good for sitcoms and romantic comedies but not so good for real life. To be fair, plenty of breakups are not a giant deal. Plenty of people do it peacefully and respectfully and go on their happy way. But most breakups are still painful. So what do you do about the pain? How do you get through a breakup and get back to normal?

KNOWING WHAT TO EXPECT

You don't have to be so confused when difficult things happen. Please know that it's good news. Because yours isn't the first relationship ever, yours also isn't the first breakup ever. Millions of other people have been there before, and they've left a clearly mapped trail for you to follow. Plus, lots of people and doctors and universities spend enormous amounts of time researching these things, also good news for you. What all this means is that your experience in breaking up and in changing, healing, and moving on is a relatively *predictable process*, and this is very good. It means you can know what to expect ahead of time (which I guess is what "expect" means anyway). When you are going through a breakup, expect five things. Yes . . . it's that numerical.

THE FIVE THINGS

> Sometimes you just have to hold your head up high, blink away the tears, and say good-bye.
>
> —unknown

When you lose someone or something, you have to grieve. Even in high school, as simple as it sounds, when I lost a football game, I would have to go through a sort of grief process before I felt fine again. I wasn't just okay right away, I'd go be by myself and go through a whole range of emotions before I was fine again. That's true for a lot of losses—lost teeth, lost keys, and lost lunch money. It's true of relationships too. The length of time the grieving process takes can vary—with teens it usually ranges from a couple of weeks to a month or maybe more depending on how they handle the situation. Whenever people lose something significant, like a relationship, there are five stages of grief they go through: denial, anger, bargaining, depression, and then, finally, acceptance. Or as the boring professionals like to whittle it down to . . . DABDA. The stages don't have to be in that exact order, but they often are, and they don't usually vary a lot.

When a relationship ends, it's like a small death. *Something that was . . . is not anymore.* You need time to grieve and to process it, not just fast-forward through the hard stuff in life. You need to understand this process, this journey, especially if you don't want it to be prolonged or repeat itself. So here are what the five stages of grief might look like in the average, suddenly ended, teenage relationship.

TR (TEEN RELATIONSHIP): MEAN OL' ERIC SAYS TO SWEET LIL' ASHLEY, "I DON'T LOVE YOU ANYMORE."

STAGE 1: DENIAL

TR IN ASHLEY'S HEAD: "No, this cannot be happening. This is wrong, something's wrong. It can't be over. I love him, and I know he loves me. This is not over."

Denial is the first stage of grief, not a river in Africa . . . get it? Fine, whatever, forget it. Anyway, in the denial stage, you just can't accept the reality that it's over. You might wonder if it's a sort of cruel joke or misunderstanding. Your life becomes centered around "fixing" this misunderstanding.

Denial is a temporary defense that says, "When I wake up, everything will be okay." It's a refusal of facts, information, and the reality of the situation. Some people can get locked into this stage, which starts a pattern of denial in other areas of life. People do this all the time, and it's a really harmful thing . . . just so you know.

STAGE 2: ANGER

> **TR IN ASHLEY'S HEAD:** "How could he do this to me? Why did I trust him in the first place? He's a jerk! I wasted all this time caring about him!"

Ashley can no longer deny that there is a serious problem she must now face. She is hurt and confused and frustrated, and also . . . angry.

When someone gets broken up with, here's some news . . . this person might get angry at some point. Anger isn't bad, by the way; it's healthy. It just needs to be expressed appropriately. The fact is people do get angry, and often. They get angry with God, at themselves, and with other people. This isn't a new phenomenon; you know this. Let's go back historically and religiously for a second. The book of Job in the Bible is the story of a guy who loses everything. He's confused and hurt and angry, just like you would be if everything you had worked for was taken away. His wife is nagging him to curse God and die. His life seems exactly the opposite of good, with a horrible wife thrown in just for fun. But that's not my point. It's kind of a weird, cool story, and they should make a first-rate play out of it, in my opinion. But my point is that anger comes from loss.

When grief enters the anger stage, people can turn to blaming others—or themselves—for what is happening. They may even start to think about "getting a little even." Neither of these are good options, by the way. There is a better way to deal with your anger. Take a walk. Get some air. Work out. Start a journal. Talk to a wise friend, parent, or pastor. Basically, figure out a way to focus on moving past the anger, not wallowing in or acting out your anger.

If you're the one who did the breaking up, and the anger is directed at you, it's important to remain calm. Keep your distance, don't let yourself be manipulated by it, and get help from others if you need to.

STAGE 3: BARGAINING

TR IN ASHLEY'S HEAD: "I'll do whatever it takes, baby. I promise we can make this work. Just tell me what happened, and we can get through this. I'll do anything. I just don't want to lose you."

Later, Ashley may pray, "This can't be right, God. It can't be. Please let this work. I'll do anything. I know I need to have a better relationship with you, and I want to, but please . . . help me, I can't lose Eric."

Bargaining—also sometimes seen as groveling and begging—is when things can get desperate, a totally embarrassing thing to be, you'll find. People may make deals with God, promises to themselves, or promises to their ex. It's during this stage that people are in danger of sacrificing their own values, beliefs, and dignity . . . anything to keep the relationship from ending. ("I'll sleep with you if it means us staying together. I love you. I'll do whatever it takes to keep you from leaving me!")

Don't do this. If you feel that kind of desperation coming on, force yourself to step away. Find someone who can help you get some perspective. Losing your dignity is not worth it. And I might add that texted begging is still begging—and people save texts. Again, think Internet.

STAGE 4: SADNESS AND DEPRESSION

TR IN ASHLEY'S HEAD: "I lost my only true love. I need sweatpants, tears, ice cream, weeping, blankets, compassion from friends, and quiet darkness . . . now! Because my *whoooooole* life is over."

When people are done denying, kicking and screaming, and bargaining, they may begin to feel sad or depressed. These feelings are not fun at all, and the person can end up . . .

- being overwhelmed by the pain and unable to think about anything else.
- going through long spells of crying, weeping, snotting, sobbing, hugging, sad movies, and more crying . . . and generally being unpleasant to go bowling with.
- having long spells of silence or alone time.
- having a loss of appetite and/or eating inordinate amounts of chocolate.
- in extreme situations, suffering from binge eating, acting out, lashing out, or hurting themselves.
- losing hope.
- dismissing God.

When the past is the past, but the better future hasn't happened yet, it can feel like you're in limbo. That better future is hard to imagine because you haven't experienced it. So you hold on to fond memories of the past—which then make you sad because the past is the past, and you don't own a time machine.

This stage of sadness and depression—believe it or not—is really important and good. Or it can be, as long as you know why it's there. You and I are wired so that we have to deal with the sadness before we can move forward. (Just don't make picture and music collections of when "life was good," because that's dramatic, slightly creepy, and it will only make you sadder.) Sadness and depression help us slow down, hibernate a bit, reflect on the past, and then slowly, slowly start to peek into the new future.

It's incredibly important to have friends, a counselor, a trusted youth pastor, or a parent around when you feel this way. Here's why it's important: It's not for pity or anything of that sort. You have literally lost a form of love and support, and you need to be surrounded by other forms of love and support to replace it for a while. This is a necessary stage, but it can also be dangerous. It's here that eating disorders, shame, deep depression, and suicide can get their momentum and strength, so it's especially important to surround yourself with people who care.

This is also the time when it's really important, *especially* as a teenager, to take care of yourself. I know this sounds simple, but when you are beaten down, you may not feel like doing a couple of the basics: eating well and exercising. But do it anyway. Make it a routine, and make it a priority. Your body has a miraculous way of balancing chemicals, feelings, hormones, and stress when you keep it healthy.

Use your mind to fight your feelings. Your feelings want you to wallow in them, but you can't. Watching a sad movie can be good—it can help you let go of your emotions. (*The Notebook*, anyone?) But watching twenty sad movies in a row is probably just going to cause agonizing and self-loathing. Just saying.

Feelings are very strong, but you aren't at the mercy of your feelings. "Fake it until you make it" is an old but true saying. Sometimes, you just have to do what you should do and eventually the right feelings will catch up with your right actions.

STAGE 5: ACCEPTANCE

> **TR IN ASHLEY'S HEAD:** "It wasn't meant to be; I know that now. It's been hard to go through, but I'm finally ready to move on. And I think I'm a better person because of what happened."

Acceptance is when you are finally able to look at the past as "the past." You can see things more clearly and not just emotionally. It begins to feel as though you are just telling a story instead of living in the battle scene of that story. You get your self-confidence back, and you even find the energy to start thinking about a better future. Acceptance is that little voice you have been longing to hear, the one that quietly whispers, "It's going to be okay." Because, after all, it is. It really is going to be okay.

SAY WHAT?

During tough times like breakups, teens (and adults) like to borrow other people's quotes and sayings about life, a pretty normal little trend. Usually it's to make their own ideas more concrete. Some of these sayings are actually pretty wise, while plenty of them are dumb and only sound wise.

WISE-ISH SAYINGS

♦ If you love something, let it go. If it comes back to you, it's yours forever. If it doesn't, then it never was.

♦ Sometimes you just have to hold your head up high, blink away the tears, and say good-bye.

♦ Better to have loved and lost than never to have loved at all.

♦ I cried today . . . not because I missed you . . . or even wanted you . . . but because I realized I'm gonna be all right without you.

♦ You have to take the good with the bad, smile with the sad, love what you got, and remember what you had. Always forgive, but never forget. Learn from your mistakes, but never regret.

DUMB SAYINGS THAT ONLY SOUND WISE

💎 Never regret anything, because at one point you wanted it. (*Ummm . . . no.*)

💎 From now on . . . when you think of me . . . just remember that I could've been the best thing you ever had. (*If he dumped you . . . he's probably not thinking of you a lot. Sorry.*)

💎 Cling to your imperfections; they are what make you unique. (*What if being a jerk is your imperfection? Yay, you're a unique jerk.*)

💎 I only follow the voice inside me. If it guides me wrong, I'll learn from my mistakes. (*This could be schizophrenia. Check Wikipedia or contact your family doctor.*)

💎 Remember: whatever happens, happens for a reason. (*Okay, but sometimes that reason is because you were dumb and not thinking.*)

Uh-Oh . . . You Got Dumped

Figuring Out the Why

QUESTION: We were so happy, why did he dump me? One day, everything was great. We were together, getting along, and in love. The next day it was over. What happened?

This is one of those not-so-easy questions. In fact, any question about *why* another person does something can be tough to answer. People can be complicated, and so are the reasons they do things. So . . . this girl says she and her boyfriend were happy together one day and it was over the next. Let's think about that. Were you *both* really happy . . . or was it just you? If you were the only happy one, then that could be a big part of the problem—maybe he was unhappy or confused, and you didn't see it. Either way, an abrupt ending without much explanation can be confusing. But usually it doesn't just happen overnight.

There are a lot of *maybes* here. Maybe he got scared. If he couldn't deal with the depth of the feelings he had for you, he may have decided to end it before things could go wrong and *he* got hurt. People do stuff like this plenty. So what do you do? That's the real question, anyway. Well . . . here's my honest answer: nothing. And most people hate this answer, but it's usually the best option. If you chase him, he'll most likely run away even faster. Be kind, but don't stalk. If he does come back around, you'll know it may have been fear that caused the breakup. Of course by then, you'll have had time to decide for yourself if you even *want* him back around. I mean, if the guy can't handle his own feelings, that's probably a sign or a flag or something. If he doesn't actually know what he wants, there's no sense in letting him repeatedly mistreat your heart.

Or maybe the guy was dealing with some other crisis or issue that had nothing to do with you. It may just be something he needed to work through on his own, and for whatever reason he didn't tell you. This is a time when one of the old cliché lines actually is true: "If you love something, let it go. . . ." And again, it gives you time to decide if you want him back.

Of course, it could just be that he didn't feel for you the way you thought he did. You might have gotten so caught up in picturing your relationship a certain way that you just didn't see what was really happening. It happens. You fell in love, and he didn't. It doesn't make either of you a bad person.

DIVIDING THE FRIENDS AND ACTIVITIES

> **QUESTION:** My boyfriend and I just had kind of a messy breakup. So how do we divvy up the friends? We go to the same school too, so how do I deal with seeing him?

When you share the same school, social group, job, youth group, running trail, or community garden, it can be tough to avoid your ex. But for starters, there is the Golden Rule. We hear it in elementary school, but it only *sounds* elementary. Treat your ex the way you would want to be treated. It doesn't matter what he did or didn't do. Be kind . . . and try to sit on the other side of the room when possible.

If it's a social thingy, or whatever, don't assume you are the only one being invited. Some of your friends will not want to deal with the whole "Who do I invite?" issue, so they'll simply invite you both and let you work it out. In a large group, this may be okay. But at a smaller gathering, this gets weird quickly. Avoid the awkwardness by just asking, "Did you invite (insert ex's name here)?" If so, don't pitch a fit. Simply give your regrets and say something like, "Oh, okay. I probably won't come, just because it's a small group, but that's totally okay." Above all, smile, be gracious, and be glad the person thought to include you. These things actually work, by the way.

KEEPING YOUR DIGNITY

Just as there are a variety of ways to mess up the break up, the possibilities for getting "breaked up, brokened up, broked up" poorly are almost limitless. Here are some things to avoid . . . for your dignity's sake:

1. ARGUING

Breakups don't have to be unanimous decisions, nor are they court battles that you can "win" by arguing your case. Besides, is that a fight you really want to win? *"You know what, sweetie doll face? You're right, I am a giant loser and I'll never meet anyone better than you. I see this clearly now. Thank you!"* This is an example of something that has never happened, by the way.

2. BEGGING

This is what you do after you lose the argument. Begging is really, really bad. So avoid this. You're better than that, or if you aren't, at least pretend you are.

3. MAKING A LOUD, DRAMATIC, PUBLIC SCENE

If you collapse in odd-sounding sobs and snot bubbles every time you run into your ex in the school hallways, you're not just embarrassing them, you're making a fool of yourself. There's absolutely no upside to this, even if you feel all bold-and-told-the-world-out-loud about it—except that people will picture you doing this to them if they dated you. Probably not super attractive.

4. GOING AFTER THE EX'S FRIENDS ROUTINE

I'm not talking about mutual friends. I mean the lame move where you try to steal his friends, talk bad about him to his friends, or even more annoying . . . date the best friend. Don't do that. It ends up being pretty obvious, and it usually backfires anyway.

5. EXACTING REVENGE

Depending on why you broke up, this can be extremely tempting. I get it. I have some third-grade axes to grind too . . . you know who you are. Unfortunately, it will usually come back to bite you, so try to resist. Revenge sounds sweet sometimes, but in all honesty it makes you creepy. Also, it increases your chances of committing odd crimes that will appear on your permanent record.

6. BECOMING A MONSTER

Keep it civil, or you'll end up looking insane. If it helps, try to remember that there were once a lot of things you liked about this person. Try to hold on to that—not forever, but just long enough to offer a sincere "Be well" (or something like that) and actually mean it.

7. AND . . .

- Don't badmouth your ex's new love interest. It just makes you look petty. Even if you're a hundred percent correct, you lose by looking jealous. And undignified. Don't say everything you think. A good self-reminder to you and me.

- Do *not* threaten to kill or hurt yourself. Seriously . . . no one is worth hurting yourself over . . . no one. Also, it's manipulative, and no one deserves that kind of blackmail. Besides, it only makes the person want to get farther away from you.
- Do not decide that all members of the opposite sex are useless or heartless because of one bad experience. It's not fair to anyone—most of all, you.
- Do not agree to one last . . . whatever. This is often predictable, with predictable outcomes, involving confusing, frowny faces mixed with tears. Don't go for the one last kiss, date, sunset-horseback-waterfall ride, or whatever it might be. It makes everything more difficult, and therefore dumber.
- Don't stalk. It's creepy, you won't make new friends, you'll have to start wearing all dark clothing and hoodies, and you really should have better things to do with your time.

GET CLOSURE

When it's over, it's important to make sure both people know it's over. If you still feel drawn to the person, that's normal—people are drawn to the things they are used to, even if they are in the past. But do try to get some closure. Find someone you can trust to give you good, sound advice—someone who will tell you what you *need* to hear, not just what you *want* to hear. Talk out all your thoughts and fears. But whatever you do, do not confide those thoughts and fears in your ex. This will only prolong the healing process and confuse you both.

Now, repeat this statement until you believe it: This breakup is only one situation in my life. It won't define my future or keep me from being happy or finding love. It may not seem like it right now, but my feelings will change as I change.

A NEW BEGINNING

Strange but true fact: how you choose to see a breakup will, in fact, make every bit of difference. The end of a relationship is really a new beginning, and people like new beginnings. They always have.

Plus, let's be optimistic here: being single is also fantastic. It gives you the freedom to do more things you enjoy without having to consider someone else's likes and dislikes. Being single also gives you time to focus on yourself. Let's be honest: relationships take up a lot of time in a day. Take that time to learn more about who you are and what you want—which will help you make better relationship decisions in the future.

Life is a series of ups and downs. And the downs don't last forever, I promise. Don't let the "downs" keep you from getting back to the "ups."

Just because you haven't experienced the future yet, doesn't mean it's not brighter than you've been imagining. Maybe it's time to start picturing a better future anyway.

chapter 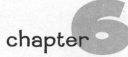6

MAYBEEEE ... LET'S WORK IT OUT

{ People don't ask for facts in making up their minds. They would rather have one good, soul-satisfying emotion than a dozen facts.

—Robert Keith Leavitt }

Do-Over, Anyone?

"Make up" is really just a clever way of saying "conflict resolution," but that's not as fun to say at all. While the specific situations vary, most conflict resolutions have the same common ingredients. Knowing those ingredients and how you should approach things can help, especially when the goal is ... well ... resolution.

STOP IT, FAIRY TALES

This is the place where we get confused: making up is not about fairy-tale endings and getting everything you ever wanted. Fairy tales are not helpful in resolving relationship issues, partly because they are mythical, I'd guess. So let's not do the fairy-tale versions of people and relationships.

To "make up" is to become reconciled.' It's something that you do, which makes it a verb. By definition it involves words like *adjust, make peace, accommodate, bring together, harmonize, integrate, settle, restore harmony, balance,* and *come to terms with.* This is much more than just "get back together with."

> Making up is not about fairy-tale endings or getting everything you ever wanted.

In other words, it isn't about getting what you want, and we forget this a lot, apparently. It's about compromise, resolution, and finding peace. It's not about being right or wrong; it's about understanding and improving. The good news for you is that if you do it right, making up will resolve conflict, heal wounds, and give you the best chance of repairing a relationship, even if it's on the brink of being gone for good. But first, you have to ask yourself . . .

BUT SHOULD WE MAKE UP?

Answering this question requires some thought and some time. Just what you wanted to hear, right? But first things first. Make sure that enough time has passed so that you're both thinking clearly. That's more than a day or two, just so ya know.

And while you're taking some time, think about the why—the real *why*—you are having a problem in the first place. Because not figuring this out is what keeps most people from being able to make up and move forward together.

Let's start with the basic question: *What's the problem?* Chances are you think the other person is the problem, and he or she probably thinks you are. And chances are you're both right, because there are two sides to every story. But in the middle of a conflict, it often becomes about one person being right and the other wrong. In order for resolution or "making up" to happen, both people will have to work together.

There's no better time to be open and honest with yourself. What are your own faults or issues? Everyone has them, so start by just admitting them. And then . . . what were your ex's faults or issues? Keep in mind, these answers are your opinions—your ex will have opinions too.

If you're the one who did the breaking up, go back to your reasons for breaking up in the first place. Have things changed enough to consider giving your ex a second chance? And if you're the one who was dumped, take a serious look at the relationship *and* at how the breakup was handled. Is that what you want out of a relationship?

You may want to write all this out on paper. Writing actually helps your brain process better in a reflective way. It gives you the time and space to complete your thoughts and make sure they are . . . well . . . thoughtful. And when it comes to deciding whether or not to make up, *thoughtfulness* is what it's all about. Okay, well, thoughtfulness and time.

GIVE IT SOME TIME

Yes, time. We don't always like this seemingly simple answer, but time is almost always essential for mending a relationship. It's fear that usually rushes things—like the fear of losing the relationship forever if you don't hurry. Don't let fear take over and make you run to your ex and resolve it all instantly. This leads to embarrassment, usually for the runner. Before trying to mend things, let time do some of the work, and just leave the other person alone for a while. Let the emotions cool off and calm down, for everyone. Give it a week, two weeks. It's not that long in the grand scheme of things, but it will improve your chances of working things out. (The exception to this rule might be if you owe the person an apology—if so, just make your amends and do it sooner than later.) Time also allows you to figure out what has *really* been happening.

HAVE THE CONVERSATION

The conversation can be tough—even though you're trying to smooth things out. It's the fear—the fear of not knowing what to do, the fear of fear, or the fear of really uncomfortable moments—that can make people dread this conversation. But if it's a conversation you need to have, don't let fear stop you, because a couple of minutes of conversation can make a gigantic difference. Plus, it will help you learn to resolve more issues in the future. So talk to the person about the situation. Be kind and honest and respectful. Ask how he or she feels; explain how you feel. Just know that whatever happens, it's okay. Remember: other people are allowed to choose whether or not they want to keep going or call it quits, and so are you.

{ You can conquer almost any fear if you will only make up your mind to do so. For fear doesn't exist anywhere except in the mind. }

—Dale Carnegie

TIPS FOR MAKING UP

There isn't a simple, one-size-fits-all, universal plan for making up. There are, however, some very good principles that can help:

☑ **Set expectations.** Begin your conversation with something like, "Hey . . . I just want you to know that I would really like to have a conversation, not an argument, just so you know my thoughts. I want to hear your point of view, and I'd like you to hear mine as well, if you're okay with that."

☑ **Don't worry about being right.** There is no such thing as "winning an argument" when it comes to relationships. You can be right and still be very unhappy . . . and also very single.

☑ **Be humble.** Seriously, be humble. Approach the person calmly and with respect. It's the right way to be with people, period.

☑ **Apologize.** If you sincerely take responsibility

first, it makes other people want to do the same. Really . . . try it; it's powerful. Just don't apologize for things you didn't do.

☑ Don't apologize expecting an apology back. You are there to take responsibility for yourself. You can hope that the other person might do the same, but you can't expect it, because that's . . . well . . . not what apologizing is. It's "I'm sorry"—not "I'm sorry, but only if you are too."

☑ Use relaxed language, including body language. Don't cross your legs or arms, stare, point, or scowl. Make sure your mouth and body are saying the same thing. *Tip: Guys do better when sitting side-by-side than face-to-face. So pick a relaxed setting where eye contact and confrontation are minimized.*

☑ Think in terms of what's best for both of you. By the way, don't tell the other person what's best for him or her; that will be completely unhelpful and might be part of the problem.

☑ Try to talk less than the other person. You want your ex to do the talking, to express things to you, and to feel listened to. That's what resolution is about. Be sure to thank him or her for sharing—and do it sincerely. Keep in mind that you aren't there to resolve everything in one sitting; you are just there to talk.

☑ Don't let your emotions take over. They can make your brain shut off, and then bad stuff happens. Making up requires lots of things, including your ability to think rationally.

☑ Affirming is not agreeing. You don't have to agree with someone to validate their point of view. You aren't saying that it's your point of view too. You are simply saying you can see things from their point of view as well. When you validate what people say, you'll find that they will listen to you more.

☑ Give the other person time to process. Don't force an answer right away—it's more likely that you'll get the answer you don't want. Think chess, not checkers.

☑ Agree to disagree. Sometimes the best way to make up and move on—together or apart—is to see each other's point of view. If both people will withhold big reactions for just a minute or two, then they can talk and listen freely instead of defending themselves. Not worrying about being right helps people get past the arguing stage.

☑ Be patient. Just . . . be patient. Be patient while you're being patient too; that helps. Trees take time to grow, wounds take time to heal, and conflict takes time to resolve.

Sooo, This Seems Like Bad News, I Know . . .

No matter what our plans for life are, they change—and not usually when we plan on them changing (ironic, huh?). But it's an important reality that we should really get more comfortable with, in spite of how all the movies about love end. Sometimes . . . it doesn't work out. No matter what you do or don't do, it may not work out. Sorry, but I mean . . . so what? You had a plan, and now it's not the same plan. It's not the end of the world, even if it's painful. Happens to just about everyone. That's why life is about doing the right thing, being honest, apologizing and forgiving, gaining clarity, and listening. We should learn to seek peace with people . . . whether or not we end up in a relationship with them.

The plans we make for life always, *always* change. They just do. But if we expect change, maybe we will get less upset when it happens. There are simply too many variables to plan a whole life in advance, so . . . don't be bad at math.

Changing plans just means you have the ability to make a better plan, maybe add new details and destinations, maybe even with apps 'n' stuff. Everyone likes apps 'n' stuff.

chapter 7

WHY IT HURTS

{ The world breaks everyone and afterward many are strong at the broken places.

—Ernest Hemingway }

PUPPIES AND TODDLERS

Sometimes you like people and they don't like you back. This always feels really good. Yay, rejection, right? Anyway, I get a kick out of puppies and toddlers, probably because they have a lot in common: they slobber, make funny noises, poop wherever they want, love people, and entertain me, in particular. When puppies and little kids don't like me, for whatever crazy reason, I feel rejected (don't judge). That might be specific to me, but the feelings of rejection are not. And the only thing worse than people not liking you back is when people don't love you back.

I know this sounds simple, but one of our greatest needs in life is to know that we are cared about, thought about, and loved by others. And when someone who has been filling that need suddenly stops, that's when the hurt begins. Rejection causes pain. Period. The real question is *why*. As in, *why* do people cause us both love and pain?

Chad,

I don't understand guys, period, but the biggest confusion about guys is this: Why does it seem like it's possible for a guy to drop someone so much easier than girls do? How can you love someone one minute and then just forget about them in a couple of weeks like it didn't happen? I get so frustrated with this, and I feel like a fool for loving someone who can suddenly not love me back anymore. Please help me understand.

—Mary Anne

Whether or not Mary Anne is experiencing actual mature love is a discussion for another time, but what she *is* experiencing is rejection, loss, and a feeling of failure. And these things hurt . . . a lot. When relationships end, break up, or just go bad, you feel real pain, much like the real pain of a shark attack or being hit by a bus (both buses and sharks hurt a lot). This pain just happens to be the emotional kind. And wouldn't you know it—emotional pain actually hurts longer and deeper than physical pain. No matter how it happens or why, breaking up can feel like . . .

Hey there, individual that I've been telling how special you are, I should let you know I've changed my mind. I know you are a real person with a heart and feelings, and you've cared about me for a prolonged period of time, but I've decided against you. Certain things are much more interesting to me right now than you. Things like my immature friends, guys who are jerks, other girls who flirt more and don't use their brains, the Internet, making jokes, sitting at home doing absolutely nothing, my lack of appreciation for good people who care about me, and getting to reject you and hurt your feelings. Take care, and try not to take it personally. I'll probably do weird, confusing things from now on, and you'll wonder why I even wanted to be in a relationship with you in the first place.

Sincerely,
The Causer of Your Tears

Feeling rejected causes an emotional reaction in us, and it's almost instantaneous. It can make you wonder, very simply, if you are good enough (you are). Then all those other fear-based feelings—like loss, inadequacy, confusion, comparison, insecurity, panic, and sadness—may pay you an unwelcome visit.

If the common symptom of a cold is a runny nose, then the common symptom of a broken heart is emotional pain. But why? I mean, why don't you also feel equally happy that you got out of a relationship that wasn't working? And why aren't you happy for the chance to find someone who will care about you more? Why do you feel the bad feelings so much more than the good ones? Some of the answers are very . . . surprising.

LOVE AND FEAR

Love is a *huge* concept—from the smallest, microcellular level of things to the largest concepts of the known physical universe and God. Our tendency, especially in America, is to define love—very quickly—by how it's shown romantically, and I think that's a big part of the confusion. There's a lot more—I mean *infinitely* more—to love than dating and romance.

If you think of love as a pie chart (and who doesn't love pies?), then most people would think it looks something like this:

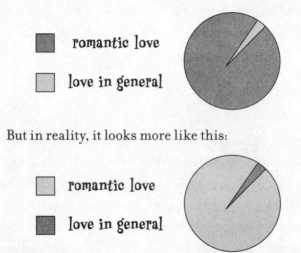

■ romantic love

☐ love in general

But in reality, it looks more like this:

☐ romantic love

■ love in general

In our culture, romantic love takes up probably 90 percent of the uses for the word *love*—according to all the romantic comedies ever made. I mean, find a story where you don't see love portrayed as mostly romantic—it's rare. The good news is that this picture of love is wrong. And, no, thinking less about love romantically doesn't make you less romantic. In reality, romantic love is a drop in the ocean of all that is love. Love is much larger and much purer than romance and feelings. Love is the most important thing in the world, after all.

> There is no fear in love. But perfect love drives out fear.
>
> —1 John 4:18

To understand pure love is tough, maybe impossible, I dunno. Because pure love is only possible when we have absolutely no fear, and we little humans are always fighting fear. Technically this also makes us "fraidy cats," I think.

Fear is the real root of why we feel pain in a breakup.

Growing up, I always heard "God is love,'" but to be honest, it was hard for me to understand what that big statement could even mean. But as I get older, maybe gain more experience in life, it actually makes more and more sense. And I think it can help us understand our relationships, especially the painful parts. If we can get theological for one moment, consider the love and God thing with me. I can't picture the whole universe, but it's very large. And if God is above all of it, then God's love is large, on a scale that is magnificent. God, being pure love, means there is no such thing as fear in his presence. No fear of rejection or loss. We, as humans, can have great love, but our love is not pure and perfect . . . So we also deal with a whole lot of fear in life by default. And fear is the real root of why we feel pain in a breakup.

MOMS YELL LOVE

There are strong psychological and scientific arguments for believing that all emotions stem from either *love* or *fear*. Fear is for protection, while love is for life's joys and pleasures.

Picture a mom who sees her four-year-old son running toward the street. Instantly, she turns on the mom-glare-stare-thingy and screams, "Stop! Look at me right now! Don't you ever run out into that street! Do you hear me?" She might seem very angry, but in all reality, her anger is a byproduct of fear. Think about it: she is *acting* out of fear for her child . . . who apparently loves cars and danger and angry moms. But mom won't stay angry. Most likely she will hug him, tell him she loves him, and then explain *why* he shouldn't run into the street. This is a small example of how *healthy fear* might work.

But in our relationships, a lot of times we don't act out of healthy fear. And because love and fear are so closely related, it can get confusing, as it does for Breanna . . .

WHAT ARE WE REALLY AFRAID OF?

Chad,

I am so confused right now. It's because of a guy, and one who used to love me. He always told me I was beautiful and wonderful, and he said he would love me forever. A month ago he said I didn't love him as much as he loved me and ended it, and then he called *me a waste of his time! I'm trying not to care anymore, but to be honest it just hurts. It won't go away.*

—Breanna

Breanna has a predicament, and it stems mostly from feelings of rejection. She has just lost love—or at least a form of love. And Breanna, in reality, is fearful that she'll never find love again. Our feelings aren't always rational, after all. Her pain then comes from both the loss of love and the fear of never getting it again.

The truth is that Breanna, like most people, will find the love she is searching for—at college, maybe in the workplace, or perhaps later in the city where she ends up living. The real danger for Breanna has nothing to do with boys. The danger is in never understanding where her feelings come from in the first place. Without that understanding, she, just like most people, will likely re-create the same situation with someone else and then be even more frustrated because "real love" hasn't worked again. Here's your psychology lecture for the day: the key is to understand where your fear comes from, why you have it, and use it to make informed decisions.

RELATIONSHIP PHYSICS

Newton's third law of motion states, "For every action, there is an equal and opposite reaction." While I'm sure the physics police will be knocking down my door, I'm going to adapt this for relationships: for every action, there *can* be an equal or opposite reaction.

If you give care, you are supposed to get care back in return, agreed? I hope so. But sometimes you give care, and then you don't get it back. At some point, we will all be in that situation. And at some point, we will all be given care but not want to give it back. This is when pain happens.

SMALL HELMET-HEAD CHILDREN

I spend a chunk of time in the hammock on my front porch whenever possible, reading or hanging out, all comfy and floating in the air. Hammocks are underrated, if you want my opinion, and I have a flowchart to prove it.

Anyway, when I'm not being sarcastic in my hammock, I like watching some of the funny stuff that happens on my street. One Tuesday afternoon, I saw the little girl who lives across the street out playing and riding her scooter. She is about four years old, her best friend is her puppy, and she looks especially funny in her big pink helmet on her miniature scooter. Little Helmet Head—or Josey—fell off her scooter and skinned up her knee pretty good. And guess what the first thing she did was? Cry. Instantly. Then she started the most dramatic walk I've ever seen, all the way back across the front yard, holding her knee in a respectably dramatic fashion, and weeping and moaning, *"Mommmyyy, huhghhh kkkmmmm bluhhh snottttt faaacce, Mommmyyy,"* or something like this. Her mom, of course, ran over, and Josey fell into her arms. And as I watched this interaction, I thought it was . . . kinda weird. Here's why:

Do you find it odd that a kid would first crave a hug to help a bleeding knee? Is it strange that little helmet-head Josey wanted emotional comfort for physical pain? It's true that a hug doesn't heal a hurt knee; however, pain is much more bearable in the arms of someone who loves us.

As an adult who doesn't need my mom's comfort as much as I used to, and who also hits my shins on tables often, my first reaction isn't to cry for my mom. In fact, these are my first three thoughts, usually:

1. *Owww!*
2. Don't cuss.
3. Where's the stupid antiseptic?

The only reason I don't cry when I'm hurt (as far as you know) is because years of injuring myself have taught me that it will probably be okay in a few minutes. I mean . . . I still need love and comfort from people, and so do you. But as we grow up, we learn to get this in different ways than four-year-olds with helmets on scooters do. One obvious way is with the relationships we choose.

As you grow up, some of the emotional needs that have (hopefully) been met by your family will begin to be met by others—whether it's in a romantic relationship or a friendship. So if one of those people suddenly stops meeting your emotional needs, it's simple . . . you hurt. While your mom may say, "I've loved you since before you were born," other people can give love and then take it back. When you lose relationships, it's like being little Josey Helmet Head, crying on the sidewalk with your knee bleeding, and no one ever comes to give you a hug and tell you it's okay. And it's not your skinned-up knee that hurts the most.

So Why Does It Actually Hurt So Much?

Because Love Is Attachment

Blame it on our DNA, if you like, but we are wired for attachment. As you start to spend time with friends and romantic interests, you become attached to them. That's because time spent together is related to feeling attached—it's the way that we become closer to people. So when the person you're attached to decides that he or she wants to be . . . well . . . unattached, it hurts.

Because You're Stuck on How "Things Should Be"

When you are dating someone, your mind creates a story—usually a story about a future that hasn't happened yet. Because you probably like your boyfriend and don't sit around imagining fights with him, then your story probably doesn't include things not working out. After all, what's the upside of sitting around imagining a breakup?

Chad,

My best friend is in love with a complete, and I mean *complete,* jerk. She's the only one who doesn't see it. It's like he has some spell over her and she can't see anything clearly. She thinks he's amazing, but he's not; he's a jerk. He treats her and everyone else terribly, but she won't listen to anyone. She just says I don't understand. How do I tell her that she's the one who doesn't understand? She's my best friend. I don't know how to get through to her! Help!

—Devon

One of the most insane things people say is some variation of "But I know who he really is!" They usually say this because other people don't feel the same way about that person. And while some may call this being optimistic, it's often a denial of reality. What a girl usually means is, "I hope he ends up as the person I think he could be." In reality, it's better to see people for who they are right now. And when that "happily ever after" story in your head turns out to be wrong, it's confusing and—you guessed it—painful.

BECAUSE PEOPLE GET TO CHOOSE

Santa Claus is not real. Sorry if that's news, I really am. When kids are around six or eight or nineteen, someone tells them that Santa isn't the one putting the gifts under the tree. And when they find out there's no jolly, obese, bearded man with flying reindeer, it usually causes emotional distress in the form of little kids' tears. I never cried, of course (I wept. But at the end of the day, it was a childish belief, and it had to change).

Our feelings about how love should be can also be childish, in the sense that they can be a younger understanding of love and relationships. Sometimes our feelings need to grow up too. Love isn't just the warm, fuzzy feeling you get when you first realize that the person you like actually likes you back. Those moments are great and all, but they don't define love by any means. Real love is a choice and a verb, not just a feeling. When the warmish-lovey-hug-face stuff fades away, that's when the choice part steps in—you either choose to love someone for who he or she actually is . . . or you don't. Of course, your lovey-dovey gets to make that same choice. So what happens when the one you choose doesn't choose you back? Well . . . pain happens, that's what.

Because Einstein Said So . . .

I don't know enough about physics to lecture about it, but here's another physics-type lesson on people. Albert Einstein once gave an example of the "relativity" in the theory of relativity by saying:

> *Put your hand on a hot stove for a minute, and it seems like an hour. Sit with a pretty girl for an hour, and it seems like a minute. That's relativity.*

And, in a weird way, this also applies to why things hurt. Time seems to pass much slower when you are experiencing pain, whether it's a broken arm or a broken heart. When things are going great with your friends or your special someone, a week can go by in a flash. But if you've just lost a relationship, that same week can seem like an eternity.

Because Your Pants Came Off

Physical involvement—particularly sexual involvement—leads to greater emotional attachment, period. And because Einstein and Newton said so (pretty sure), the greater the emotional attachment, the greater the pain in a breakup.

Very simply, the touching of the private goods will connect you to someone more than not knowing them that way. Sex is one of the most natural things on the earth. It's about love, respect, closeness, pleasure, making babies, life, and bonding. As a Christian, I find that God's view on love and sex, when you break it down, is really smart, romantic, and much needed. If you think about sex happening with two people who desperately love one another, bought rings, made vows, and strive to live in love, you can see how it is a very beautiful thing. The thing is, this isn't the picture of sex we are usually given. When people have sex as young, uncommitted, and unmarried individuals, they usually break up shortly after (four weeks is the average for teens), and they don't enjoy sex as much either. What you also find is that their description of love is more often a description of a *lack* of love.

The wisdom of keeping your pants on isn't meant to be about rules; it's an actual, tangible boundary that protects people, especially the heart parts of people. It's a way to minimize the potential emotional pain in your life until you can be smarter about how to give and get love. It also avoids disease and pregnancy, so . . . win-win. I really do believe the wisdom in the literature of the Bible. For example, Proverbs says, "Above all else, guard your heart, for it is the wellspring of life" (4:23). And you know what? That's very real, and very smart, advice.

Plus, as far as teen sex is concerned, can I just be very up front with you about this? Seriously, not kidding, and I swear to you . . . it's way overhyped, people are awkward, it doesn't work out like it does in the movies, and you really aren't missing out on much. I have way too many letters and e-mails from regretful teens.

BECAUSE RELATIONSHIPS ARE PART OF YOUR IDENTITY

How tall you are, your hair color, your eyes, your family, and your voice are part of your basic identity. Now add hobbies, your sports, your clothes, your friends, your music, your "style," and the people you like and the people who like you, and you'll see part of the next level of your identity. So when people who help make up part of your identity change—or leave—it can leave you feeling lost, confused, frustrated, and in pain.

BECAUSE PEOPLE WHO HATE DRAMA ACTUALLY LOVE DRAMA

One of the more frustrating reasons breakups are so hard is because of the drama. And the truth about people is this: some people prefer pain to no pain in life . . . enter the classic "Drama Queen." And, yes, there are some "Kings" out there too, but we don't really say Drama King now, do we? To use a female example, the drama queen is often an addict, and her drug of choice is pain. A simple clinical definition is this:

> *This addiction is not really to pain, but primarily to free-flowing endorphins—a hormone-like substance that the body releases whenever a pain or injury is experienced. These endorphins accompany the pain and are very similar in structure and effect to the opiates, like heroin and morphine.*[2]

And, yes, I just compared drama queens to heroin addicts because addiction is addiction—the drug just changes. Just don't go telling any drama queens that I said they're a heroin addict. I do *not* prefer the drama, and I'm certain of it.

Put simply, drama comes from pain and then causes pain. But it also fulfills a need. Dr. Eric Berne and Steve Karpman note clearly in the acclaimed book *Games People Play* that "in all drama there needs to be a victim."[3] If you know someone who is constantly tangled in some drama, then you'll also notice that person is usually the victim in the drama. This isn't a conscious, intentional decision, but it's also not a coincidence. As odd as it may sound at first, and without getting too psychological about it, people often create situations that give them the positive or negative feelings they need. Take Sydney, for example:

Hey Chad,

I'm going out with my best friend's ex-boyfriend, and he really hates her, so now she hates me. She has another boyfriend, but she still likes my boyfriend. I can't hang out with both of them together without him glaring at her and saying mean things. They aren't going out anymore, and I hate all this drama. What should I do?!?!

—Sydney

Really, Sydney? Odds are that this isn't the only drama Sydney finds in her life. Sometimes when a person tells me she has drama in her life and she hates it, I'll say something like, "Let's be clear: if you say you hate drama but you have a lot of drama in your life, then you don't hate drama—you love drama."

Of course, if I said that to Sydney, guess what would happen . . . she'd get all dramatic about it. Go figure. She would probably be so hurt that anyone would even say something like that! Of course, that's the perfect scenario for her because she becomes the victim once again.

Here's a thought: healthy people listen to the information

being presented to them, consider it, and then agree or disagree. Victims feel first and then usually disregard what you
are saying in order to become a victim again.

"Out of the overflow of the heart the mouth speaks"
(Matthew 12:34) is pretty much the same thing you learn in
Psychology 101. We don't consciously make every decision in
our lives, but the decisions we do make reflect our past experiences, fears, desires, and motives. When drama pops up in
your family or in other situations you have little control over,
that's one thing. But when you have recurring dramas in the
relationships you pick, then you picked those relationships
for a reason, even if you didn't know why. So if you are the
drama king or queen—take a step back and honestly examine
your actions. Maybe it's time to take off the crown.

ICEBERGS

Roughly 80 to 90 percent of an iceberg rests underwater,
depending on which ocean it's in and other factors. The
equation for this has to do with the density of ice (0.9167
g/cm) compared to the density of salt water (1.025 g/cm).

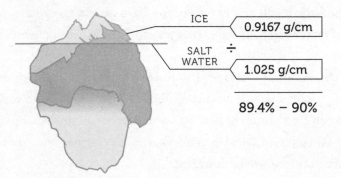

ICE — 0.9167 g/cm

SALT ÷
WATER — 1.025 g/cm

89.4% – 90%

Now that you know this valuable information, also know this: people are kind of like icebergs; sometimes we are only seeing the visible parts on the surface, not the big parts below the surface. People have all kinds of stories, and we don't know what they have been through.

So a Little About Me . . .

I spent a year and a half of my life locked up in a long-term correctional facility and drug rehabilitation program. I know, I know, it *does* sound awesome, you're right. But in those couple of years, I got more therapy than a vampire-obsessed teen girl will need in the future. I mean . . . love with pale, dead vampire-y peeps? That takes some therapy to get past.

One thing I learned in therapy (that wasn't sarcastic) is that people get more addicted to the *feelings* that come from drugs or relationships than the actual drugs or relationships themselves. And when people get addicted to negative feelings, that's when they start to constantly find themselves in bad situations and relationships. Here's one explanation: "The emotional pain addict consciously or unconsciously seeks out such situations that will surely result in pain."[4]

If I didn't want to get punched in the face, I would absolutely find a way to avoid getting punched, especially in the face. It stings and you look dumb. And if people really didn't want drama, they would put a lot more effort—and brain usage—into avoiding drama. Our behavior usually speaks more clearly than our mouth does.

LET'S GET SELF-HELPY NOW

Pointing out *why* something hurts doesn't necessarily make someone feel better. Sorry about that, really. But knowing *why* is the first step in helping it not hurt. So what *do* you do about the pain?

For starters . . . start simple. Breathe . . . and then know this: healing takes time. You might be in emotional pain for a little longer than you would like, but you will get through it. And as you do, you'll realize that there are important life lessons in pain, if you will consider them. Here are a few things to help you get through it.

ALONE ISN'T LONELINESS

Feeling alone because you are missing certain people in your life is absolutely normal. You need people around you, but just as importantly, you need to resist the urge to run to people and completely distract yourself.

YEAH, YEAH . . . DO ROUTINE THINGS

When you are hurting, you aren't as physically or emotionally motivated to do the things you would normally do. So while routines can sound mind-numbingly boring, they are also incredibly important. They provide a basic structure for your time and can help balance out painful feelings. Exercise, for example, creates a host of positive reactions for you, including more dopamine in the body, which is the thing that makes you *feel* happy.

It might sound like cheesy self-help at first, but plan some quiet time in your routines. Take time to hibernate, ponder, take a walk or a yoga class, or read. Once again, "fake it till you make it." Sometimes you just have to keep doing the right things as you wait for the right feelings to catch up.

Say No

When you are in pain, you simply aren't able to help others in the same way you normally can. Learn to say no kindly but more often. You need time for yourself, to understand and process things.

Stop Being an Island

While it's important to spend some time on your own, it's equally important to spend time reaching out to others. John Donne, a famous poet, once wrote, "No man is an island." This is true; we are all very much connected—or at least we should be. But when people are hurting, they can tend to close themselves off on their own tiny island.

I myself am a small island, and probably you are too. But alone, we all are very limited. Honestly, I know that any ten random people together on an island will be better off than me on an island by myself, with no one to talk to but some fish and my sunburn. My problem, and maybe yours too, is that we believe this very strange idea that pops up sometimes: "I can do it by myself." But you know what? I can't and neither can you. I need people, you need people, we all need people. Yay for people, and let's just admit this.

It's just not good for us to live life alone. If you're alone on your island, start sharing it with people. You'll find that a lot of people have been waiting for someone to build a bridge over to their island, and they'd gladly do the same back. They just need someone to do it first. Personally, I'd rather live on an island chain with a lot of people. There's always gonna be a beach bonfire at some point. And who knows, maybe s'mores. Be an optimist.

THINGS HURT BECAUSE THEY HURT

Difficult things hurt; they just do, and it's still going to be okay. Kicking the corner of a table, or a porcupine, hurts. So does breaking up—whether you've dated for a couple of days, a couple of months, or a couple of years. Pain isn't always bad, it's just painful. And sometimes you just have to get through it. You have to hang in there, but . . .

it *will be* okay, and things *will* get better.

1 2 3 4

{ Your Two Minds }

IDIOTS AND GENIUSES

{ Nothing in all the world is more dangerous than sincere ignorance and conscientious stupidity.
—Martin Luther King, Jr. }

Chad,

My relationships have been really bad the last couple years. The guys I pick are the same types of guys I've always been drawn to, and no matter what, they always end up cheating on me. I find myself becoming obsessed in relationships, and I lose my identity when I have a boyfriend. Can you help me? I'm really confused and don't know what to do.

—Christina, a functioning teen
girl, not considered an "idiot"

Chad,

I have a problem. I keep getting hit by cars. Whenever I run into the middle of the highway, just to get some exercise, a car always hits me. I don't ask for it, and I always scream at them not to hit me, but they don't listen. Why is this happening to me? I just want exercise, and I keep getting hit by cars. I don't know what to do!

—Idiot

Hmmm . . . do you see any similarities between the letter from the "non-idiot" and the "idiot"?

I have been writing books and traveling nationally to speak with young people for the last eight years straight, and there is one phrase I hear *allll* the time: "I don't know what to do." Here's the thing about this little phrase: it seems innocent enough, but it actually hints at a much larger problem. Now, to be fair, it's a really admirable trait when you don't know what to do and you ask for help. You can't know everything, after all. Asking for help isn't what concerns me. What really concerns me about "I don't know what to do" is this: What if you do? What if you actually do know what to do?

IDIOTS ARE EVERYWHERE

So that you don't hate me . . . I'm not using *idiot* the way it might immediately come to mind. The word today is commonly a slang term and is usually combined with words like *dumb* and *stupid*. But that's not actually what it means. In both its Greek and Latin origins, the word *idiot* did not, in any way whatsoever, refer to someone with low intelligence. By definition, being an idiot happens when people forget the skills and knowledge they already have, or when they simply choose not to use them. Which means that being an idiot is optional . . . just so you know, which is really good news.

So when I use the word *idiot*, I'm actually talking about someone who behaves "in a self-defeating or significantly counterproductive way."[1] And let's be honest, we are all idiots at one time or another, and some of us often. Sometimes the way our minds ignore important and obvious things is just . . . idiotic. For example:

Chad,

My boyfriend and I have been dating for a few months. He doesn't really talk to me. He just keeps me at a distance. He says he really likes me, but he's so nervous and quiet and won't really ever tell me anything that helps me understand him. I don't know how to help him. When I talk to him about this, he just says, "Hey, this is who I am. Sorry if you don't like it." I know something else is going on. How can I change this? I have tried so many things, but nothing works. I care about him and want us to have a good relationship!

—Angie

I don't want to sound harsh toward Angie at all, because she genuinely believes that she wants to make things better in this situation. However, Angie is doing something that all of us do, and we're all idiots (proper definition of *idiot* here) for doing it. She is choosing to believe the illusion—and the delusion—that she can change another human being.

The catch is that our friend Angie actually knows a lot of things. She reads books, goes to school, knows precalculus, and drives a car. She also knows these pretty authenticated facts: gravity exists most places we go, bears aren't for hugging,

> Pretty authenticated facts: Gravity exists most places we go, bears aren't for hugging, and *you can't change other people.*

and *you can't change other people.* But she is ignoring the fact that you can't change anyone but yourself. The problem in Angie's situation is not, repeat, *not* her boyfriend or his shyness or his lack of communication. He very well may be ignorant of how relationships work, but it's Angie who has the real problem. In fact, here's a list of Angie's (and a lot of other people's) oversights in this situation:

- seeing what you *want* to see in people, and not what's really there
- telling someone else how to behave and then getting frustrated when he doesn't do what you say
- imposing your values on others
- idealizing your relationship
- creating a parent-child relationship (strange, but it happens . . . a lot)
- trying to change someone else before you change yourself

- trying to change someone else
- even thinking that you can change someone else
- walking up to a brick wall, kicking it repeatedly, and then crying about why your foot hurts and is all bloody and broken and whatnot

So you know, this is just your basic starter list. There are thousands more examples. And this doesn't just apply to dating relationships—these are good to remember in any relationship. And then there is this letter:

Chad,

My friend is guy crazy and is making so many bad choices. She is drinking and will do anything for older guys to like her. I try to tell her what she is doing is dangerous because I care, and that she doesn't need to do this, and that she is amazing the way she is, but she doesn't hear me. How can I get my friend to understand this!?!

—Katie

Katie is thinking a lot like Angie—but in a different kind of relationship. If you have a hard time watching or accepting other people's choices (I struggle with this), then you might fall into the category of people who mix together three-parts caring with a pinch of idiot on the side. You can *hope* other people do good things, and you can *expect* them to do good things—especially when it relates directly to you—but you cannot *make* people do good things. And to think you can is, well . . . delusional.

{ I not only use all the brains that I
have, but all that I can borrow. }
—Woodrow Wilson

TURN YOUR BRAIN TO "ON"

This whole "idiot" idea might sound drastic, maybe even insensitive, but I really don't think it is, and here is why: all the confusing topics surrounding teens—boyfriend/girlfriend confusion, drama, breakups, sex, and a general confusion about how to evaluate people—really hint about a bigger, more complex problem. That is, *people often assume they are helpless, even clueless, before they even wonder if they aren't.* Read that sentence again; it's important.

Fact: millions of young people ask questions they already have the ability to answer. Okay, yes, maybe you don't know the *exact* answer to a specific question, but many times you already have all the basic information you need to figure it out. Like in math—you may not have the answer to a specific problem when you start, but you do have the basic formula to figure it out. Relationships really aren't that different. Your brain works just fine; you just need to use it.

REACH FOR THE STARS, JUST NOT GREAT RELATIONSHIPS ?!?

In our country, we are constantly reminded of all the things we can do if we put our minds to it: reach for the stars, accomplish our dreams, be anything we want to be, all that stuff. You could probably list twenty more sayings from every classroom poster and inspirational movie you've ever seen.

So, if you can reach for the stars . . . then you can learn about people too, right? Well, that's where things get weird. Do you remember seeing any of these quotes on a classroom poster or in a heartthrob, lovey-face movie?

> You can do amazing things; relationships are one of them!
> You can understand yourself!
> You decide your happiness!

Maybe you've seen some of these sayings, which seem odd, but I sure haven't. So, why? The reality is that people kind of lose their minds when they get in relationships. I was told I could be an astronaut more often than I was told I could understand girls. Even the saying "Reach for the stars" is—if you want to be weirded out—really a way of getting you killed. I mean, stars are millions of degrees hot and you have to go to space to get to them . . . where there is no oxygen, which humans are "super into." Also, I'm pretty sure I'd need a space shuttle, and at $4 billion a pop, that's not looking great. So, if I reach for the stars, I'll really just be standing in my yard with my arms in the air, weirding out my neighbors again, untll I feel hopelessly reminded that I won't even reach a treetop. Great advice, teachers; thanks a lot. The alternative, though, "Find realistic, attainable goals according to your opportunities, skill set, and geographic location, then educate yourself in order to achieve them!" just isn't as catchy. I'll work on that.

> Common sense is not so common.
> —Voltaire

The point is this: when you *aren't* told that you can have great relationships, or that the quality of those relationships is choice over chance, why would you think differently? What if "You *can* have great relationships" were drilled into your brain instead of "Reach for the stars"? Many people expect relationships to be difficult and full of struggle. Not coincidentally, the people who believe this tend to find relationships full of difficulty and struggle. We *can* do the relationship thing better than this.

Wait . . . Your Brain

Logically, you know that effort is a big part of getting what you want—you learn that in first grade. The more effort you put into something, the better it turns out. You also know that there *are* happy people, great relationships *do* exist, people go through tragedy and *go on* to become even greater because of it, and plenty of people *decide* their own outcomes in life. You can't *not* know these things if you have looked around at all in your life-time, or if you just have the Internet. And if you are a Christian, you also have lots of guidance and wisdom, passed down for thousands of years. Stuff like . . .

I can do everything through [Christ] who gives me strength. (Philippians 4:13)

Wait . . . relationships are things!

So I turned my mind to understand, to investigate and to search out wisdom. (Ecclesiastes 7:25)

Wait . . . we can get wisdom?

For wisdom will enter your heart, and knowledge will be pleasant to your soul. Discretion will protect you, and understanding will guard you. (Proverbs 2:10–11)

That sounds kinda neat, like a force field or something . . . maybe.

Do not forsake wisdom, and she will protect you; love her, and she will watch over you. (Proverbs 4:6)

The Proverbs writer gives a beautiful description of wisdom using personification. Grammar geeks, anyone?

You're Not an Idiot at All

Do you really believe that relationships are so confusing that they require some sort of secret knowledge or advanced degree? Do you really, deep down in your heart, believe that guys will always be confusing, that girls are crazy, that guys and girls will never understand each other, or that relationships break your heart, are too hard, and never last? I've had a few difficult relationships too, but I don't believe they are all that way. Sure, girls can be complicated, but so can guys. Relationships can be difficult . . . check, got it. But you know what else is true? Rockets are super complicated and involve rocket science, but you can learn to build them. Learning calculus is really hard, but most people could do it. Finishing a full triathlon is one of the most challenging things a human can do, but thousands of people do it every year. You could probably finish a triathlon if you really wanted to, which is most likely optional. It would be hard training, but you could do it. And you *can* understand relationships and learn to have a good one—it just requires effort and knowledge. No magic formulas, no super-secret handshakes.

ELEMENTARY, WATSON

A good relationship starts with ourselves. Reminding yourself that you really *are* a smart, capable person (because you are) changes your brain almost instantly. Give this idea a chance. Read the following letter. But don't read it as you normally would; instead, read it as though you're a brilliant and famous detective, Sherlock Holmes maybe, standing in a room full of clues. Your mind takes in every clue—on the surface and below it—to figure out what's happening and what to do about it. Ready? Okay then . . .

Chad,

So I really like this guy, but he likes my best friend. She likes him a lot too, and he wants to ask her out. Because he's my friend, he asks me if *he should go out with her. I keep wanting to tell him that he shouldn't, but I'm afraid he will know it's because I like him. I really want to tell him how I feel, but without hurting my friends. Please help me.*

—Courtney

I picked Courtney's letter for a reason: it's a little simple, a little immature, and a little overly dramatic. This doesn't matter; you'll still use the same skills for answering these questions as you would for more complicated ones. Let's consider a few things:

What are the basic facts of the situation?

_____

_____

_____

_____

What is Courtney's real problem?

_____

_____

_____

Is Courtney's problem really that confusing? No, it just requires using your brain and not acting all helpless and saying, "Help me! I don't know what to do!" This is what I see when I read this letter:

- First, Courtney likes guy romantically. Guy likes other girl romantically. Other girl likes same guy romantically. Other girl is Courtney's friend. No mention of guy liking Courtney back romantically.
- Second, Courtney is not asking what either of her friends wants. She is thinking only of herself (always a bad sign) and what she wants—even if it hurts her friends.
- Lastly, Courtney is trying to control what other people do and how they feel.

So, what do you think the answer is to Courtney's problem?

_____

_____

_____

_____

_____

Here's what I would write to Courtney if I were being simple and blunt:

Courtney,

I imagine you are sweet and mean no harm in this situation. But seriously . . . stop it. You have two choices here: either be happy for your friends or hurt them. You are making this all about your feelings and forgetting theirs. Two people like each other, and you are trying to ruin it for them. Just because you like someone, doesn't mean he has to like you back. Don't sabotage people for any reason—especially not your friends. Your actions will just end up hurting you. So go enjoy your day . . . you aren't ready for relationships just yet. You'll get there soon enough.

—chad

PRACTICAL WISDOM

Aristotle lived a very long time ago. He didn't go to prom (pretty positive), but he did note some fascinating ideas about life, which is why we all still know his name. One thing Aristotle noticed was that architects had only straight rulers to measure length. This was a problem, however, when measuring columns and other round stuff. Then, Aristotle noticed that the stone masons came up with a flexible ruler, made from lead that could *bend* around the column and measure its circumference that way, thus "bending the rule" to accomplish their goal. Which, of course, is where the saying "bending the rules" comes from. Aristotle called this ability to take existing knowledge and create a new solution with it "practical wisdom." It's the ability to flex and bend your mind to find the solutions in life.

We need "practical wisdom" in our lives, and plenty of it. Saying "I don't know what to do" before you've tried many things is not flexing the gift that is your brain, which probably makes God sad since brains are neat and complex and useful, and because we are really capable—sometimes we just forget.

If you can reach for the stars, then you *can* understand people and have good relationships. The first key to this is knowing your own mind.

Well, more accurately . . . your own *minds*.

YOUR TWO MINDS

Whatever any man does he first must do with his mind, whose machinery is the brain. The mind can only do what the brain is equipped to do, and so man must find out what kind of brain he has before he can understand his own behavior.[1]

{ He is a double-minded man, unstable in all he does.

—James 1:8 }

DOUBLE-MINDED

Your body feels; your mind thinks. *That* is actually the order in which things are supposed to go. Your feelings move you, and your mind thinks. Remember that. It's important. And yes, there may be a test. But probably not.

Please read the following letter. You'll actually be reading it twice in this chapter. But for now, simply read it and just see what thoughts pop into your brain.

Chad,

So there is this guy that I like. He goes to my school and the same church too. I just moved here a few months back, and I'm pretty nervous in new situations. I really like him, and he's really cute and is nice to me, but I am too shy to talk to him, and I freak out when he comes over to talk to me. I try to make small talk about what's going on at school or whatever, but I am freaking out inside, and my sentences are stupid. I know I seem like a weirdo to him when he's really just trying to be nice to me. What if he likes me and I mess it up by getting all weird? Do you have any advice to help me get over this?

—Brooklyn

Take a second and jot down whatever thoughts popped into your head about Brooklyn and her dilemma.

_____

_____

_____

_____

_____

_____

_____

"Two minds are better than one." You've probably heard that before—or something like it. And yes . . . two minds are better than one, but *only* if they are working together. If they aren't working together, and each of them wants to be "right," then they will become enemies—which is completely not "better than one." This isn't just a saying either. It describes me, you, and pretty much everyone else on the planet. Because as it turns out, you don't just have one brain steering the SS *You* ship—you have two.

I know it might sound strange at first, but the fact remains that you have two very distinctive minds inside your brain: the emotional mind and the rational mind. They are both real, and you need both of them in order to fully understand your life. This two-minded approach to life, in fact, answers many of the questions about why we do what we do.

THE BARE BASICS

THE EMOTIONAL MIND

Human brains—and most animal brains—have an emotional mind. The studies of the emotional mind are called affective science and affective neuroscience.[2] Your emotional mind includes mood, emotionally driven behavior, decision making, attention and self-regulation, and of course, emotions. *Sooo* . . . it's kind of a big deal. I mean, just look at all those fancy words. This emotional mind of yours is made up of two specific brain areas working together: the *amygdala* and the *hypothalamus*.[3]

Chad, why are you giving me a biology lesson? Okay, well . . . since you asked nicely, these areas control most of your emotions. Here's what they do:

- The *amygdala* stores and processes long-term memory and emotional reactions. It's also the "watchdog" for your physical surroundings, using the five senses to gather information and look for threats. It then notifies your body with feelings.
- The *hypothalamus* is concerned with *homeostasis*, or maintaining the *status quo*. It regulates hunger, thirst, responses to pain, sexual satisfaction, anger, and aggressive behavior. It also regulates things like pulse, blood pressure, breathing, and response to emotional circumstances.[4]

Okay, Chad, so what do I do with this information? Well, for starters, know that your emotional mind keeps you alive and breathing, which is kind of a big deal to you. It's also your alert system—it uses emotions to "cause action" in you. You feel frightened so you jump, you feel happy so you smile, and so on. Your emotional mind collects all your life data, stores it, and sorts it so that it can be used in the future. It does way more than this too, but before we get to that, let's meet your other mind.

THE RATIONAL MIND

Your rational mind is what makes you different from a squirrel—well, that and the food you eat, furriness, and a tail.

Like the emotional mind, your rational mind "lives" in certain parts of the brain—mostly the frontal lobe. Think of it this way: if your brain were America, then your frontal lobe would be in the White House, making the important calls for the country.

The frontal lobe is developed through life experiences and just plain growing up. Children don't fully use their frontal lobe—the rational mind—and this is why they are psychotic, miniature people who cry and laugh instantly, dance, spin in circles until they throw up, and share their ice cream with the dog.[5] We all start with an emotional mind, but the rational mind develops later in life. The word *develops* is important, because it is something you have to do—and not everyone bothers to do it. Do you know any adults who seem to be on a constant emotional roller coaster? They could probably use a little more frontal lobe development.

> {
> Few are those who see with their own
> eyes and feel with their own hearts.
> —Albert Einstein
> }

The rational mind is the reason we are called "the thinking species." It balances out the impulses of the emotional mind. The important thing you really need to know is this: the better your two minds work together, the better your life will be.[6] Here's an example of the two minds working together:

Recently a girl named Katherine was telling me about her longtime boyfriend and, specifically, how he was not her boyfriend anymore. After three years together, he told her that he needed to be single and "find himself." A week later he was dating another girl. I asked Katherine how she was feeling, since it had been a couple months since the breakup. "I don't really care anymore," she said. "I'm a lot happier with my friends, and there's a lot I've learned about myself." As she said this, I noticed a tiny tear welling up in the corner of her eye. At that very moment, she was reflecting her two different minds. While it was clear that her emotional mind still had sadness and hurt from the experience, her rational mind was busy explaining the benefits of the change and choosing to focus on the positive things that came from it. Both of these things were very real and happening very simultaneously.

It all boils down to this: the rational mind thinks, and the emotional mind feels. The problem for you is that our culture values "feelings" a whole, whole, whole lot more than being rational, especially when it comes to relationships. But it's a problem you can easily overcome if you'll just use your brain. Both of them, that is.

FEEEELLLINGZZZ

Here's a strange thing to realize: many of the things you do every single day aren't really your choice . . . which is actually super-good news, I swear. From now on, when you think about the word *emotion*, think of the word *automatic*. You may not be aware of this, but emotions are mostly an automatic response, and not your choice. They have less to do with the heart, and way more to do with the *limbic (or brain) system*.[7] Yes, I said limbic system, and I know it's completely unromantic sounding.

But you know you secretly want to learn about the limbic system, so don't even act like you don't.

Picture this: You're sitting at your desk in class. Someone walks to the front of the room with a baseball in his hand. He turns around, looks right at you, winds up his arm, and throws the baseball right at your face. What do you do?

Answer: Move!

Of course you move! Hopefully extra fast because baseballs hurt. Moving would be instinctive and automatic. In a split second, your amygdala kicks in, your muscles tense, your pupils dilate, you take a deep breath and then stop breathing momentarily (this increases your vision and hearing), you make the facial expression for fear, adrenaline rushes to your arms and legs and then moves your head, neck, and whole body—hopefully out of the way—all while not screaming, if at all possible.[8] Can you imagine wondering what brand of baseball is being thrown at you? Probably not. You don't have time to worry about the details of baseball logos when the logo is aimed at your facial area. Handling details, like brand recognition, is not your emotional brain's job.

What just happened in this scene is incredibly important, and here is why: when you realized someone was about to throw something, you actually had an *emotional reaction*. It was an emotional reaction first, not physical, as most people would believe.[9]

The emotional mind—your feelings—is first and foremost a personal alert system. The emotional center of your brain is more directly connected to your eyes and the spinal cord, which connects to your arms and legs. This is why emotions affect your body so quickly.

If a bug lands on you, it causes the emotional reaction of fear or panic, which is then followed by the physical reaction of swatting, kicking, yelling, running, jumping, and generally impersonating a crazy person. The rational mind isn't present, just the spastic, nervous emotional mind. This is why we panic and are able to think, even for a moment, that a tiny bug is trying to murder us. Luckily, bugs don't know how to make fun of us for how dumb we look, mostly because bugs don't have a rational mind. Joke's on you, stupid bug, even though you can't get jokes.

These simple examples of "quick reactions" help explain why people do odd, harmful, or dramatic things in moments of conflict, stress, and anxiety. The emotional mind makes us aware of our surroundings, whether it's with positive or negative feelings, and urges us to react. But it's up to the rational mind to make sense of all those feelings—so that we don't overreact.

Be a Team Player . . . or Look Insane

Let's say you're walking down the street and you suddenly hear footsteps running up behind you. You hear heavy breathing and look over your shoulder to see a grown man running directly at you. Within thousandths of a single second, your emotional mind kicks in and sends the message, "Danger! Panic!" Your heart rate accelerates by ten beats in one second as your body prepares to either sprint from or fight this threat. (PS: These first reactions are not really your choice.) And this is when your rational mind kicks in, adding lots of details to come up with other possible answers, such as:

THINKING MIND: Hey, wait a tiny hundredth of a second. I see more things here. This person has on running shorts and shoes. He has an iPod. He is running in a straight line and breathing heavily but regularly. His face shows no signs of aggression or hostility. In fact, I've seen people who look like him before, in movies, on my street, all over. This person is casually running, not running to attack me. If I just step over about a foot, I bet he'll keep running right past me.

This is a simple but literal example of how the brain combines knowledge from the emotional mind and the rational mind to make a decision. It also reveals a simple equation, which you can apply to your relationships as well. It looks like this:

$$\text{initial feelings} + \text{factual details} = \text{a more accurate view of reality}$$

YOUR LIFE AS AN ANIMAL

The prefrontal cortex is located in the frontal lobe of your brain, and it does all kinds of very, very important "life stuff" that you may not be aware of. Stuff like:

- sort through conflicting thoughts
- determine good and bad, better and best
- determine the consequences of current activities by predicting the outcome
- control the desire for immediate gratification

- deny immediate gratification for a better, longer-term gratification[10]

The prefrontal cortex helps you push stop, pause, and *Wait one second!* before you react. This is the part of your brain that allows you to move past impulses for instant gratification. People who struggle in the whole prefrontal cortex area pursue instant gratification even while knowing the long-term effect could be bad (think drugs and sex)." And just so you know this . . . the ability to wait for a reward is one of the single most important abilities of the adult mind. It's this area that parents are referring to when you hear them say, "Use your brain, Bobby!" Technically, Bobby could yell back, "I can't completely use my brain, 'cause it doesn't finish developing until I'm between 22 and 26!" It could hold up in court . . . just saying.

If you didn't use the "thinking" side of your brain (which has to be developed) and only used the emotional side of your brain, then your whole day would be incredibly awkward and funny and also miserable. Any jogger, unpleasant feeling, or loud noise would, quite literally, send you into a panic. You would constantly be fleeing the scene, hiding, screaming, fighting people who startle you, and generally looking like an idiot. Actually, you would act more like a deer, mouse, cat, or any other animal that relies almost exclusively on its instincts.

Thankfully, the human brain is much more complex than the animal brain, which also means I'm smarter than the squirrels that live in my front yard. It also means that they won't ever understand that I'm not trying to kill them, and I want them to be my tiny, front-yard pets. If they would just get a more developed brain, squirrels wouldn't be so dumb. Our uniquely developed brain makes our lives amazing, and also more difficult, which is why it's important to learn to use both your minds. After all, you don't want to go through life and relationships acting more like a nervous animal than a human being. That'd be nuts. (I am so sorry about that. I had to do it. Squirrel joke thing . . . you understand.)

> Sure, listen to your heart, but then quickly add the rest of your brain.
>
> —chad

Even Back Then

The Bible's Old Testament is where you find the Ten Commandments (Exodus 20:3–17). These ten laws gave, among many important things, a set of moral guidelines for how to treat each other. Sociologists and historians have noted that most of the commandments have to do with verbs that are emotionally based: "You shall not *murder*," "You shall not give false testimony (*lie*)," "You shall not *steal*," and so on. Here's the really interesting part to me: if emotions are, in fact, meant to "move" us, then even the Ten Commandments can be seen as a way to help guide people's emotional lives—which apparently they had a hard time doing even back then.[12] Some things seriously never change.

WHY EMOTIONS EXIST

Let's talk about our feelings some more. I mean, who doesn't love talking about emotions all day? Besides me. So, to get historical about it, the word *emotion* comes from the Latin *motere*, which means "to move."[3] To put it simply, emotions literally exist to cause action in us. They are the alert system that screams, "Hey! This could be important! Pay attention!"[4] That's *why* emotions exist—as a sign to pay attention and use the rest of your brain. It's when we forget that whole "use the rest of your brain" part that we get into trouble.

The emotion of fear can cause you to immediately spring up and run from a falling tree, and that can save your life. You wouldn't process the situation of a falling tree. You would either hear a branch break, or you would see it breaking. Then your emotional mind would cause you to react to danger more quickly than you could "think yourself to safety." In this way, emotions serve a very good and simple purpose, to help keep us alive. On the brighter side of things, when someone makes you happy, you feel happy, and your brain makes your mouth form a smile, almost automatically. This sets off a chain reaction of chemicals in your body and generates a soothing, calm, and contented feeling in both people—in you and the person you're smiling at. Why do you think when someone is happy that it makes other people happy? Our bodies and mind crave soothingness and contentment and pleasure. Happiness really is contagious, and now you can prove it.

WHAT FEELINGS DO FOR YOU
Here are some cool—and good—things our emotions do for us:

☑ ANGER: Blood flows to the hands, making it easier to grasp weapons and fight. The heart rate increases, rushing hormones and adrenaline through the body and allowing for quick, strong movement.

☑ FEAR: This is the danger sensor. Blood is diverted to the skeletal system, mainly the legs, which can leave the face pale and cold. The body prepares for fight or flight.

☑ HAPPINESS: Brain activity increases and actually blocks out negative feeling centers, giving a greater sense of calm and productive energy. Happiness is a state of rest, and it allows for enthusiasm and readiness for upcoming tasks.

☑ LOVE: These very soft and "tender" feelings are the physical opposite of fear and anger. Love is the "relaxation response" and generates a state of calmness and contentment, which allows for cooperation.

☑ SURPRISE: This is primarily a visual thing. Is that surprising? (So, so sorry.) It's expressed by lifting the eyebrow, which takes in more visual scenery and allows light to strike the retina. (Did you mimic a surprise face just now?) This allows the eye to take in more information to figure out what is happening.

☑ DISGUST: Disgust curls the upper lip to the side and wrinkles the nose at the same time. This looks the same in every culture on earth, and they never even had a meeting about it. Biologically this suggests that we are trying to close our nostrils to a bad odor, or to spit out food that might be poisonous. In other words, when we look at people with disgust, it's a way of rejecting them, almost like their words or ideas are poison. So . . . think about that for a minute.

☑ SADNESS: It is important; let's make that clear first. Feelings of sadness indicate loss, and it's the emotional state that helps people adjust to loss. This might be a letdown or a breakup or the death of a loved one. Energy levels drop, and there is little enthusiasm for movement. In other words, sadness causes us to withdraw. This withdrawal "creates the opportunity to mourn loss, grasp its consequences for life, and, as energy returns, plan new beginnings." That means sadness serves a real purpose.[15]

THE TRUTH ABOUT BEARS

If a bear stands on two legs, it's not threatening. It stands up so that it can see better and take in more of its surroundings. You'd be surprised (again, so, so sorry) to know that it is less likely to attack while doing this, because it is actually mentally processing all that it is seeing. I saw a very large bear do this once in the wild. I can't say that this info helped much, though, in that I still wanted to pee and cry at the same time.

WHY THIS MATTERS FOR YOU

When you are angry or infatuated, overwhelmed or craving something, it's because your emotional mind has a grip on you. It connects first to your physical senses, and it can cause your body to react more than your mind is ready for. In other words, you have to connect your emotions to your rational mind—it won't automatically happen. And if you don't, these things can happen:

- frequent feelings of urgency or anxiety
- a failure to self-monitor
- reacting without thinking, impulsiveness
- giving up quickly
- thrill seeking without thought of the consequences

EMOTIONAL HIJACKING

> Chad,
>
> I have a guy problem, as you can guess. I was 16 and started my relationship with my first boyfriend. For two years it was really good and I thought that nothing could go wrong and we would be together forever. Then one Saturday, at the mall by the way, we sat down and I could tell something was wrong. I could feel something bad about to happen, and my heart started to pound, and I got really, really overwhelmed and couldn't breathe. He told me he was breaking up with me and said it would be better if we didn't talk at all. I had a breakdown in the mall, right in front of him, and I was humiliated. I didn't feel like I had any control over my feelings, and I had to call my mom and have her come pick me up. I'm so embarrassed, and it's made everything worse. I don't know what is wrong with me, but this isn't normal. I literally couldn't even control myself, and I felt humiliated. I still do. Please help, Chad. I don't understand any of this, and it's making me hate myself.
>
> —Marilyn

What Marilyn doesn't know is that her "humiliating" response was really the result of her emotional mind running off and leaving her rational mind. She was emotionally hijacked. Her emotional mind felt fear and anxiety, which made her physically react as though—in the most basic sense—her boyfriend was going to attack or harm her. Her emotions told her body to hide, fight, or run.

Now, imagine if Marilyn—or you in a similar situation—knew this information ahead of time. She may have started to have the same reaction, but then could stop and "rationalize." She might have been able to say to herself, "I'm freaking out emotionally, and my emotions are telling my body to freak out physically. I need to calm down." And then . . . she could. And so could you. It starts that easily. Once you know what's happening, your rational mind can put it in perspective so that you don't end up the victim of an emotional hijacking.

Strong emotional reactions aren't always a bad thing, by the way. You can also be overwhelmed with laughter or joy, like a laughing fit or crying tears of joy (probably more gals than guys on that one). It's the same bodily reaction; it's just centered around positive emotions. People should strive to freak out in these ways more often, in my opinion. It's like super good for your abs too. Just a side note.[16]

IF YOU DIDN'T HAVE THE EMOTIONAL MIND

The emotional mind is odd sometimes, but the bottom line is you wouldn't really be "you" without it. Your emotional mind is the passion center, awareness and social center, and the store place for your emotional memories. When people have damage to the emotional centers of the mind, especially the frontal lobe, they behave more like a zombie than a "real person." They prefer to be isolated from other people. They lose recognition of feelings and can't remember close friends or family. In essence, without your emotional mind, your life would not have personal meaning. You might know that you are alive or that you want food, but you wouldn't ever wonder why you're alive or enjoy the taste of ice cream. You also wouldn't care about other people in your life or be able to laugh or cry, and that's kinda sad in a way. Not being able to cry kinda makes me want to cry—and luckily that's a sign I don't have brain damage.

THE SERIOUS CONSEQUENCES OF NEGLECTING YOUR TWO MINDS

If you are only rational and don't listen to emotion, it's bad. But if you only listen to your emotions and neglect the rational, that's bad too. This is why:

Letting your emotional mind take control will lead to a *whooole* lot of things that you don't want. Like panic, frustration, anxiety, and feeling overwhelmed and in pain longer and more often. You will feel *more*, while being able to *do* less about those feelings.

Feelings are amazing, and incredibly important, but only if they are paired up with knowledge. The more significance you place on emotions, the less you place on combining knowledge with those emotions. This is why we see people who are slaves to their emotions. They believe *their* feelings are stronger, and they often think others simply don't care as much as they do. This isn't true, of course. You'll also see patterns of "Why do these things always happen to me?!?" echoing throughout their relationships. The most likely answer to this (however simple it may seem) would be . . . "These things happen to everyone, but the rest of us deal with it correctly and learn to move on quicker than you." Those who are controlled by their emotions usually fall into one of two categories:

- PESSIMISTIC PEOPLE: These are the Negative Nancys, and too often, they can become cynical. They are more likely to feel angry, stressed, threatened, and emotionally hurt than others. The why is simple: they feel a negative emotion, and instead of working through it, they let it snowball.
- CONSTANT CRISIS PEOPLE: Emotional flooding is what happens with people who are consistently carried away by their emotional brain. Their heart rate jumps, while their body pumps adrenaline and floods them with stress. The result is a self-induced crisis. Simply hearing the words "We need to talk" can cause them to lose the ability to think clearly. This crisis state is incredibly addicting, and the longer people do it, the harder it is to stop.

ANGER IS DANGEROUS

Anger is okay; it's healthy even. But "undealt with" anger causes rage. To put it another way: anger says, "I'm angry," while rage goes and gets a bat. The fact is, you will either control your mind and your emotions in life, or they will control you. Right now, you may not see how these things matter so much in your day-to-day life, but in fact, few things matter more in your day than learning to control your two minds. There are consequences when the two minds don't work together. And it's only when people neglect their rational mind that things like drama and abuse and shootings and other horrible things are possible.

THE VOICE OF REASON

Take a look back at Brooklyn's letter from the beginning of the chapter on page 140. Read it again, this time keeping in mind the information we've been discussing. Do you see anything differently? Is your picture about what's happening any different knowing that there are two minds she is getting messages from?

You can probably see now that a lot of Brooklyn's feelings come from those exact same things we've been talking about. Her body is getting one message about the situation from her emotional mind, while her rational mind is telling her it's okay and good and healthy to be having a conversation with a nice, cute boy.

Look back at the thoughts you jotted down the first time you read the letter. What do you think about it now?[17]

_____

_____

_____

_____

_____

Be Clear-Minded

The struggle between our two minds is not a new one. Centuries ago, the philosopher Plato wrote about these "mental unbalances" we all struggle with, and he used a pretty accurate example to do it. He compared the mind to a person riding in a chariot pulled by two horses. The person holding the horses' reins is the rational mind, while the horses represent the emotional mind—all our desires and appetite for life. It's important to keep those horses under control and to not let them be in control. Otherwise, the horses—our emotions—will run wild. And horses like to run wild, after all. Then bad things happen, like crashes and broken chariots. Metaphorically speaking, of course.

When head and heart are balanced and used properly, they help with guy stuff, girl stuff, stress, conflict, love, fear, loneliness, worry, happiness, joy, and so on. You can think and feel more clearly, and things are just better in life. When head and heart are out of balance, that's when confusion and frustration set in, and you will not be able to "think straight." You don't want this. It's a terrible way to live, there's no reason to, and it insults your capable mind.

Here's the gist of it: your rational mind needs guidance from your feelings, and your emotional mind needs to be guided by logic and reason. This combination of heart and head is known as *emotional intelligence*. It makes your intellectual intelligence higher and might very well decide "how well you do in life" more than anything else. It applies to *every single aspect* of your life—from faith and love, to friends and family, to careers and children.

This is wisdom, in a biblical explanation, and the Proverbs writer says, "He who gets wisdom loves his own soul; he who cherishes understanding prospers" (19:8). That's a good thing. People don't really seek wisdom out often enough, but for those who do . . . it's well worth the reward.

1   2   3   4

{ Moving On }

chapter

MOVING ON: PART 1

{ Even if you stumble forward, you're
still moving forward.

—unknown }

{ If we want change, but we refuse
to change our own minds first, then
we will be slaves. Slaves to the past,
slaves to our former selves, and we
will never change.

—chad }

THE POINT OF BEING A TEENAGER

The point of being a teenager is to change. Really, that *is* the main point. You change from a child to an adult. In between, you're a "teenager-adolescent-constant-change-in-progress" version of you. Sometimes this much changing in a short amount of time can be rough. Good news: you aren't alone—almost everyone else is struggling too, even if they are good at hiding it.

The obvious changes are physical. But you also change mentally, socially, and spiritually as you start to form your own opinions about life and all the stuff that goes into it. That is to say (without playing dad), you have to develop your own independent, thinking brain.

If you look around, you'll notice that a lot of people exchange the privilege of using their own mind for someone else's easy answer. This is terrible for people. Please, do *not* do this, because it will hurt you. It's critical to learn to figure out the answers to life's problems for yourself. Why? Well, take a look at Monica's situation:

Chad,

I am graduating from high school soon. My boyfriend has waited seven months on me, he loves me, and we want to sleep together, but I don't know how I really feel about it or him. I love him, but I don't think we'll be together in college, and I'm afraid I'll end up regretting it. What should I do?

—Monica

The answer to Monica's question is "Don't do it." Very simply, very clearly, "Don't. Do. It!"—for a hundred different reasons, maybe more. There's the emotional bonding, the disease risks, the fear of pregnancy, and all of the relationship complications that come with sex in young and uncommitted relationships. Monica probably already knows this. The problem is that Monica doesn't seem to know why she should say no, even though part of her knows she will regret it, which means she doesn't know how she got to the answer of no in the first place.

> Borrowed brains have no value.
> —Yiddish Proverb

One of the most critical skills in life—not just relationships—is learning *how* to figure out the answers to your questions. And that means putting some thought and effort into your decisions, along with some knowledge. Simple answers are great, but they're not what life is about. I could just give you a bunch of answers for your "how to get over a breakup" questions, like: "Take some time for yourself, girl," or "Don't text him, no matter what!" And while those general answers are good answers, life isn't about just accepting someone else's answers. You need to be able to use your brain to find things out for yourself. If you don't learn it now, you will not magically understand it later. The evidence for this is everywhere in young adults. Do you really want other people making the big decisions for you? It's your life, after all! So, move on with it.

LIFE'S A JOURNEY (YEAH, I SAID IT. BIG DEAL.)

Think about moving on with your life—after a breakup or any other hard time—as an intense journey, perhaps like a month-long backpacking trip. And like any journey, it's going to take knowledge and effort if you want to finish. I mean, you don't just grab some Cheetos and sandals and head out across a large desert. That's silly, mostly because Cheetos are silly, and deserts are big. Also, you don't want to run out of food, have to quit early, or accidentally die on your journey. It's super embarrassing when you accidentally die on your own journey, and you don't need humiliation on top of failure. So, yes, this "moving on" journey can be a challenging one. The destination is worth it, though, I promise. You are on a path—with no exaggeration—to a better life. First thing you'll need for your journey is a map. After all, it's important to know where you're going and what to expect along the way.

Your Map

The map for your journey will be written by your own mind, so you'll want to be careful which ideas you use to make the map. Nobody wants a confusing map; that's how people get lost in the woods and end up getting eaten by a bear, because bears are all sneaky like that.

When I really want to move on from something in my life, I know I need a general direction to move in and some rules to follow. By the way, I have learned what works by first doing it all the wrong ways, so learn from my mistakes, okay? A basic map that I use for any life journey looks something like this:

Chad's Map for Traveling to the Future

Stop and evaluate my surroundings · Be deeply honest · Search for wisdom · Begin again using what I have learned.

This journey process starts in my own mind and nowhere else. I use my mind to look at the world inside of me, and I use this very same mind to see the world that's outside of me. How I use the information my mind gathers will decide if my life finds more clarity or more confusion, more love or more fear, more happiness or more discontent. This requires both self-awareness and self-responsibility, and I usually have to repeat this process several times to find the best new path. But when I need to move on from something, I know that my mind-set matters more than anything else. In the end, my thoughts shape my feelings, my feelings shape my desires, and my desires shape my life.

Your Guide

Feelings can act as a guide for the journey, but—and this is a *big* but—feelings can lead you down the wrong path. Feelings *can* and *will* hurt you if they aren't combined with a very particular part of your brain—your frontal lobe.

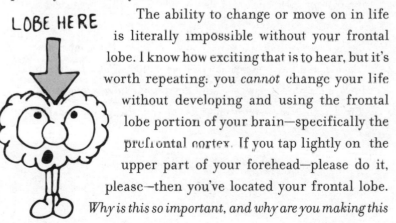

LOBE HERE

The ability to change or move on in life is literally impossible without your frontal lobe. I know how exciting that is to hear, but it's worth repeating: you *cannot* change your life without developing and using the frontal lobe portion of your brain—specifically the prefrontal cortex. If you tap lightly on the upper part of your forehead—please do it, please—then you've located your frontal lobe. *Why is this so important, and why are you making this book about brains and biology, Chad?* Well, talking about neuro-science may not seem like it would help with moving past a lousy lost love, but consider this: from your teen years until your midtwenties or so, your frontal lobe is going through a crucial development phase. The frontal lobe is the last part of your brain to be developed, it's used for higher reasoning, and it's what makes you an adult on the mental level. Unlike the other parts of your brain, your frontal lobe has no interest in what you *have* been doing. It could care less about friends' names, shooting a basketball, or food cravings. Your frontal lobe is too busy being concerned with your future—which is what makes it so important in the moving-on process.[1]

GETTING UNSTUCK AND ON YOUR WAY

Chad,

How do I ever change if I'm stuck in the same place with the same people? No one ever tells you how to do this, because it's impossible! I pray and try to be nice, even to the people who are being so mean and rude to me. They remind me of the mistakes I made, and I can't escape my past no matter what I do, and it makes me want to give up. Am I doing something wrong, or is there just no way to move on when you can't escape your past?

—Kylie

Kylie just can't seem to get herself unstuck, even though she wants to. Even worse is that the more she tries and doesn't succeed, the more of a toll it's taking on her. Her letter shows a common struggle for young people, and that is learning to combine her head and her heart when planning real change. Kylie has to nurture a new way of thinking if she ever expects to put her past behind her.

Kylie's letter also shows the awkward phase of the developing teen mind. Flexing and stretching your mind is just like flexing and stretching a muscle—it's exercising it that makes it bigger and stronger. As you learn to flex and use your frontal lobe more, the answers to your questions will become easier to see. In essence, you and your frontal lobe have to team up to move forward.[2]

> You know you've got to exercise your brain just like your muscles.
>
> —Will Rogers

The question becomes this: Do you really want to move on and to change? If so, look at the following list. Do you need to change or move on from any of these things?

- a broken heart
- bad relationship(s)
- loss of someone close to you
- guilt and shame for past decisions
- loss of reputation or self-esteem
- constant drama

- shallow friendships
- bullying
- depression, anxiety, insecurity, or fear
- bad decisions about sex, smoking, drinking, porn, and/
  or drugs
- sexual abuse, rape, incest, pregnancy, or abortion
- bulimia, insomnia, or anorexia
- divorce, emotional abuse, neglect, or abandonment
- pretending to be someone you are not

I know there's a lot on that list, and that's not even a complete list. But you'll probably find that one of the things sticks out to you, if not several. And you know what? That's completely okay. These are life's issues, and everyone runs across at least a few of them. However, don't get stuck in them. The great news is that if you are willing to do the right things, you can move past any of these issues.

HEADING OUT WITH HOPE

Dear Chad,

My dad is an alcoholic and has mentally abused me for a long time. I live with my mother, and last I heard, he was in rehab. I hate having all this hurt and anger in my heart. Could you give me advice on how to forgive him and move on?

—Sydney

Chad,

I've always had a boyfriend, ever since I was twelve. (*Side note: this is insane!*) You are right about not needing a boyfriend to have an identity, but I keep running back to guys for attention. I know it's wrong, but I guess it's hard not to do the same things over and over when you live in the town I'm from. Any suggestions that might help?

—Kelcie

Chad,

I don't know where to begin. My father was killed in front of me when I was young, and he took me on a drug deal with him. I've always been in trouble and done drugs. Counseling has been good, but I still don't know how to do things differently. Nothing has worked, and I guess I don't want to be messed up anymore, but I don't know how to not be.

—Walker

These letters show some of the very real issues teens are faced with every day. Actually, they are issues teens fight with. Because if you want a meaningful, happy, and joyful existence, you have to fight for it. You really do, by the way. And for this fight, you need hope.

Hope is believing that what you want in life can actually be had. Hope says things can always change for the better. Hope says your past is not your prison. People can go through terribly awful things and somehow be more amazing in spite of them. Personally, this gives me hope too. And believe it or not, hope is found in the strangest of places sometimes. Take Hawaii, for example. Because you always need hope, even in paradise.

Hope on a Surfboard

Ah, Hawaii. I like Hawaii a lot, a whole lot, which makes me like most people who have ever gone there. But there is tragedy in paradise too. Take the tragedy involving Bethany Hamilton, for instance. Most people know the name Bethany Hamilton. But the reason people know her name is *not* because she was a shark attack victim; it's because she didn't *stay* a shark attack victim.

By the age of thirteen, Bethany was one of Hawaii's top female surfers. I've grown up with surfing, and if you happen to know anything about the Hawaiian surf culture, in particular, then you'll know it's in a class of its own. Bethany was a very uniquely gifted athlete, the kind who just doesn't come along very often in a sport. Then . . . tragedy struck. In October 2003, in Kauai, Bethany was lying on her board out in the water when a large tiger shark attacked her, taking off her entire arm, right below her shoulder. She was finally pulled to shore but lost sixty percent of the blood in her body. It was a miracle that she even survived.

So . . . this is why her story is so incredible to me person-ally. I have actually surfed where Bethany was attacked, and I know about tiger sharks (they give me oceanic nightmares). And the thing about surfing is, very simply, your arms give you tremendous leverage and balance. I can't even imagine drop-ping in on a thick, heavy, Hawaiian wave with one arm tied behind my back. And I definitely can't imagine doing that with the memory of a shark attack in my mind.

But Bethany didn't just imagine surfing those waves again; she did it. Within less than a month of losing her entire arm, Bethany was surfing again. And then within a couple of months—not years—she was competing again. *Professionally competing*, not just surfing with a friend on a quiet beach. I think it's remarkable where hope is found. And sometimes . . . just sometimes . . . hope is found in a blonde, teenage girl on a surfboard, who should feel hopeless . . . but who is smiling instead.[3]

Bethany's story inspires me. But what really kind of puts it in perspective for me is how she talks about wanting her expe-riences and her comeback to point people to God.

Her story is a reminder to me that real faith in God brings joy and happiness and hope, even in the face of tragedy. It's this hope that matters, because it can't be taken away, and it fills people with love. And we need more people who are filled with love, just in general, always.

{ May the God of hope fill you with all joy and peace in believing.
—Romans 15:13 ESV }

KEEP GOING

We all make mistakes we don't want to carry with us. It's just reality, being a human and whatnot. You may need to get over a breakup, change the "bad luck" in your life, stop hating yourself, leave an addiction behind, find someone who can really see your feelings and heart, stop letting people use you, or find *real* love this time. Many people really do try hard to change these things, by the way, but it's not easy. And if you don't know how to go about it, you can end up right back where you promised yourself you'd never be again.

The good news is that when you know what to expect on a journey, it gives you a better chance of reaching your destination. As you learn to fully use your mind, cope with difficulties, get over hurdles, and develop real-life, critical thinking skills, then you'll finally start having more control over your future. And when you learn to harmonize your heart and your head, your journey through life will get a lot easier, and your purpose will be clearer. I swear this is good news, whether you believe me or not.[4]

So let's keep moving on into this change territory. You'll like it. The only weird thing is . . . you might have to permanently "get rid of" your best friend, if you know what I mean. Which . . . you probably don't.

MOVING ON STILL . . .

> In three words, I can sum up everything I've learned about life: it goes on.
>
> —Robert Frost

GOOD-BYE, BEST FRIEND

This may be news to you, but you should know you have a close friend who is trying to keep you from doing better in life. Let's say "she" is really less of a close friend or a "best friend" and more like a "jealous best friend." This friend knows you really well, and you have made years of memories together. But there's something about her that just isn't quite right. She never makes any new friends, and she gets jealous when you do. Let's get this jealous friend a nickname—Habit. Here's the CliffsNotes version of your relationship history with Habit:

You've known Habit for several years. You two met and quickly started hanging out together—*all* the time. Unfortunately, you and Habit haven't been getting along well lately . . . ever since you got fed up with the way things have been going for you.

Habit is from the same town you live in, has the same friends, isn't going to college, and doesn't plan on ever leaving your hometown. She likes things the way they have always been and doesn't see any reason to change. Lately, Habit has been really annoying, always talking about the past, being dramatic, hanging out with shady people, and getting upset if you disagree with her. Eventually you decide you need some new friends. One day at school you do, in fact, meet a new friend. Her name is Change.

Change is the new kid at school. She's a little quiet, but really friendly, a good student who learns quickly, and the kind of girl who has big plans after high school. She likes to watch documentaries, is starting yoga, travels a lot in the summer, and is constantly looking for new things to do. Change isn't the most popular kid at school, mostly because she doesn't seem as interested in the "same old conversations" that people like Habit are still having.

Change doesn't need attention to be happy, and she enjoys dreaming of her future. One day, you realize: you like Change. You like the stuff Change does and the way she thinks. You see that Change actually knows how to prepare for her future. Change . . . is actually the best friend you've been hoping for.

Heeeeeere's the problem, though: your past. Some friends, especially your friend Habit, really hate Change. Habit thinks Change is dumb, and Change doesn't really care for the stuff that Habit loves. Because of Habit's jealous nature, she starts trying to sabotage your new friendship with Change. Habit wants you to come back to "the way things were."

Friends like Habit are actually *frenemies.* And you have to leave your frenemies behind you, or you can't be better friends with Change. Luckily, Change is the friend who really cares about you. So feel free to kick Habit out the door . . . with both feet. Here's how . . .

START BY EXPRESSING YOURSELF

Edward Bulwer-Lytton (this English guy from the 1800s) wrote, "The pen is mightier than the sword." And it's very true. So try picking up your pen—it's remarkably useful, and you are writing the story of your life, after all. Never underestimate the power of putting your thoughts and feelings on a page. It's helpful, I promise. Just try it . . . you have to do it to see how it helps. Whether it's painting, writing, or journaling, find an outward expression that can reflect what you are going through inside.

Girls tend to be better, on average, at processing things using words, especially "feeling" words. It's culturally and biologically easier for girls at younger ages to connect words with their feelings. But writing is just as beneficial for guys too, and fellas should try it more often.

Growing up, I never really liked to write. It's strange to think that if I would have kept that same feeling toward writing, I wouldn't be sitting here at this moment doing it. Now I find that writing is therapeutic and absolutely vital for me. Plus, writing is private, and you can be brutally honest with yourself. You smell that pen on paper? That's the smell of good cheap therapy right there.

SAVE THE BIG SPEECHES FOR THE MOVIES

It's important to get all the hurt and anger out, but in a safe way. In fact, I highly recommend writing letters to your ex *that you don't actually send*. Writing gives you a chance to say all those things you want to say without screaming in public. Because screaming in public is not good. It's awkward. It makes people nervous, and they call the police. Also, it never really works out like it does in the movies. I mean, the reality is that your ex may refuse to stand still while you "let him have it." People with working legs tend to wander off when they're getting screamed at.

SAY WHAT YOU NEED TO SAY

Another huge benefit of writing is this: you can say exactly what you need and want to say. Here's the reality: talking face-to-face with someone means you have to think on your feet—and fast. That usually doesn't go very well, especially in stressful situations. Communicating important thoughts and emotions, clearly, is incredibly difficult to do in conversation the first time. Writing helps you slow down your thoughts and process your emotions more thoroughly, and it allows you to get your words just right. As a side benefit, you'll learn more about words. Plus, and I don't mean to be rude here, but have you guys seriously stopped caring about language? I mean . . . dude . . . it's bad, and I can't believe I'm lecturing on grammar. Thanks for making me feel old. But also, writing makes you a better communicator, a more introspective person, more empathetic, and more attractive, *and* it makes you smell like cinnamon, rainbows, and cookies. Scientific fact, look it up.

BEING THANKFUL

It's important for you to start seeing things more positively. Looking on the "bright side" can become a good habit. The opposite is also true. Being cynical is a habit too. So don't just write about the bad stuff; write down the *good* stuff that happens to you each day too—because something good happens every day, even if it's just not feeling as bad or someone saying something nice to you. Eventually more and more good stuff will start to happen, and your mind will be more aware of it when it does. That's a secret of happy people. Happy people don't concern themselves with all the things that are going wrong or all the things they wish they had. They are thankful for all the things—or the one single, tiny thing—they have.

GETTING ON WITH MOVING ON

As you move forward into the unknown future, there are things you will need to do in order to *keep* moving forward.

You'll be tempted to slow down or turn back at times. Don't. The future is in front of you, so just remember . . . to remember . . . to keep going.

THE FORGIVENESS FACTOR

Forgiveness, very simply, is a sign that you have accepted reality—embracing what you can control, leaving what you cannot, and centering yourself back to love and optimism in life. There really is no better way. Forgiveness isn't something you do for the other person so much as it is something you do for yourself. Forgiveness lets you heal, and you can't move on unless you heal. So . . . forgive.

CHANGE SOMETHING

You'll find that many advice books go with the angle of "give yourself a totally new you with a new haircut!" and self-empowerment sayings like that. My problem with that is . . .

1. As a guy, I don't relate to that advice in several ways, and
2. While it serves a purpose, getting your hair done is no magic pill for learning to change.

With this said, however, when you need to change inside, it can help to change things on the "outside." Maybe it is your hairstyle or your room or whatever—just nothing too drastic. This probably isn't the time to jump into the world of tattoos and interpretive animal dancing or stuff like that. I mean . . . just a thought. But *do* change something. Even a small change will cause new feelings to exist, which will help you move on from the old ones.

HOBBIES ARE A GOOD THING

Take up a new hobby or dive deeper into one you already enjoy. Yes, that sounds like a classic "self-helpy" statement. But you know what? Maybe we *should* learn to help ourselves a little more, ya ever think of that? Practically speaking, hobbies also take up time and help keep you from thinking about you-know-who-what's-his-face.

GET RID OF RELICS

Put away pictures, keepsakes, and other things that remind you of the person you are trying to move on from. Constant reminders just keep you bogged down in the past—you know, that place you're trying to escape from. So don't think about it. Just get rid of them.

GET SOME ZZZS

Play around with the idea of getting better sleep. Stay away from LED screens and other visual stimulants late at night. People who get up earlier and get better rest are more productive and healthier in hundreds of ways. Rested people think more clearly, which is always important. Also, night is a more emotional time, and that's when those sad and painful memories tend to surface. When you stay up late, your brain is too tired to deal with them clearly. There's a reason so many idiotic choices happen at night. Our brains are like batteries—they get worn down, process slower, become more emotional the more tired they are. So at the risk of sounding like your parents, all I'm trying to say here is . . . get some rest. Tomorrow's a big day. And sweet dreams or whatever.

If You've Changed Some Stuff Already, Keep Changing

When you are forced to change from a significant routine in life, it's easier to keep changing because the ball is already in motion. So there's no better time to try out some new routines and habits. Give it a shot. Start with food and knowledge, that's what I say.

START EATING WELL. Good eating helps balance out your body and your mind. Plus, you just plain feel better with better nutrition. Period. It's weird that we don't all really embrace this, 'cause it helps.

GET SOME KNOWLEDGE. Read—try some nonfiction even. Watch some documentaries, whatever it takes to learn new things and flex your mind. Make it a habit to learn at least one new thing each day. Start changing your life by changing what you know.

You Are Not Your Mistakes

{ Mistakes are a great educator when one is honest enough to admit them and willing to learn from them. }

—unknown

I want to remind you of something . . . and maybe it's something you need to be reminded of: you are *not* some mashed-together collection of your mistakes. Don't ever forget that. Really, please don't. Too many teens beat themselves up, tear themselves apart, and even take their own lives because they think their mistakes are who they are. *You are not your mistakes.*

There is a famous poetic statement in the Old Testament that says we are "fearfully and wonderfully made." And this means that you are neither a mistake nor a collection of your mistakes. We all make big and terrible and selfish decisions and mistakes. We can also move on and grow from our mistakes. They don't need to dictate the future.

{ I praise you because I am fearfully and wonderfully made. }

—Psalm 139:14

If you thought of yourself as the character in a story, the story of your life, you would start looking at that character differently than you probably look at yourself. You wouldn't worry about messing up so much, and you wouldn't be afraid that one mistake would ruin everything. Why? Because everyone knows that the main character in a story has lots of ups and downs; it's how they grow. One mistake isn't the end of the story. You know that the character can change, can become a better person. Just as you can change and become a better person. So if your life is a story, a change of perspective in the story can literally change your life.

You aren't chained to your past, and your history doesn't need to write your future.

chapter

HOW NOT TO MOVE ON

{
We gain strength, and courage, and confidence by each experience in which we really stop to look fear in the face.

—Eleanor Roosevelt
}

I was in detention ninety-six times in the sixth grade. And please don't judge . . . it's not like I got a hundred detentions. If I were to jot down some of the phrases I heard over and over in my younger school years, the most common one would be, "Chad, don't do that." For some strange reason, I personally had a hard time with that one. But there is a lot of wisdom in the "don't do that" messages of life. As you move on from a breakup—or any other difficult thing—there are several "don't do that" things that are good to know and to be reminded of.

Don't Get Tattoos When You're Six

When you're a kid, your parents do a lot of your thinking for you—or at least they're supposed to. If they don't . . . stuff can happen—like a six-year-old getting a tattoo of a milk shake and fries on his back. (*No . . . for real!*) The thing is (*and I'm not making a judgment here about any specific parents*), you really shouldn't let a six-year-old do things like that. Not because I care to tell parents what to do, but because the odds of that kid wanting that tattoo on his back when he's twenty-five are astronomically low. So according to the "commonsense handbook of parenting," if a child wants fast food tattooed on his back, the parents should get comfortable with saying, "No, you shouldn't do that."

{ The difference between stupidity and genius is that genius has its limits.
—Albert Einstein }

Not getting tattoos when you're six probably isn't a struggle for you. But when it comes to other pieces of "don't do that" advice in your life, it can be more tricky. In particular, in the moving-on journeys of life, there are some "don't do that" things you need to know. But first . . .

Facts About Us Humans

- We have feelings.
- Our feelings drive our thoughts.

- Our thoughts decide our actions.
- Our actions end up defining who we are and how we feel.

Now here is just one tiny example of how this might play out:

HUMAN BOY TALKING TO HUMAN GIRL: "I'm breaking up with you."

REACTION OF HUMAN GIRL: Within 0.3 seconds of hearing these words, her brain tells her body to start reacting—without any permission from her. Brains can be rude like that. Immediately the amygdala produces a surge of chemicals that set in motion a chain of events. Her body temperature rises as a huge wave of feelings hits, including fear, panic, anxiety, and a sense of being overwhelmed. Then the adrenaline kicks in and prepares her body for danger. (In fact, her body responds in much the same way that it would if she were about to be attacked by a bear. Seriously, it's weird.) Her brain will instantly remember all of her life experiences with other guys, how they talk to her, how she expects them to behave, whether or not they've told her the truth, and whether or not this reminds her of her father. Her brain then tells her body to respond in one of several different ways, depending on the person and her past experiences. All this happens in about two to three seconds. Odds are,

the average teenage girl in this scenario will do one
of the following:

• become overwhelmed and cry
• get angry and raise her voice
• go into a "fight" response with yelling, slapping, or
  erratic behaviors
• shut down, stopping most or all verbal communication,
  avoiding eye contact, and going into a defensive,
  almost childlike posture with her head down and arms in
• beg and plead, saying and doing whatever it takes
  to keep from accepting the fact that the breakup is
  happening

These reactions aren't necessarily wrong—you should
know that. Instead, think of them as natural—even if they
aren't a good idea and usually have a bad outcome. I mean, you
may *naturally* want to eat dozens of cookies if you're hungry and
they are placed in front of you, but it isn't a good idea. So when
your body and mind want to freak out, try to remind yourself of
these things *not* to do:

• Don't panic.
   Take a deep breath and keep telling yourself this fact:
you will get through this, and it will be okay. Being calm and
collected is a better way to figure things out, get things
done, and interact with others. Panicking is bad for your
health and everyone else's, and we do *not* need any more
problems with this country's health-care system, am I right?
Anyone?

> { Stupidity is a force unto itself.
> —unknown }

- Don't get all "reality TV" on someone.

    Pretty much everything that reality TV shows display about relationships, drama, jealousy, whatever . . . is awful—and it's meant to do this very specifically—so don't do what they do. I don't really care if that offends, because those shows really offend me. They are about drama, jealousy, conflict, TV ratings, and most importantly (to them) . . . money. People trash the idea of what good relationships mean, and they use competition, jealousy, and insecurity against people, and it's wrong in the most basic of ways.

- Stay away from the gray.

    Gray is the worst color ever when you are breaking up. Don't wear it, say it, spray it, or whatever else you do with gray. I mean *gray* as the "half relationship" thing. It will just confuse you; it always does. If you are breaking up, make a clean break. Delete phone numbers, take down pictures, put away or get rid of anything that reminds you of the relationship for a while. It's not being weird or extreme—it's making a clean break. *It's a breakup already!* Gray is an emotional snowstorm that you'll just wander around in, being lost and cold. If frostbite is your thing, awesome. If not . . . don't wander around in it. A lot of people get lost in there.

189

• Don't try to be friends right away.

Your head may know you're broken up, but your heart may not—especially if you're trying to be friends with your ex. There has to be a period of separation in order for your heart to clearly get the message. So break up all the way, which is what breaking up is anyway. Friendship, if it's possible, is for later . . . much later. So how can you tell if you're ready to be friends with your ex? Ask yourself this question: if you heard that your ex was dating someone else and was very happy, would you be able to be happy for him? If not, then you're not ready to be friends, because friends are happy for their friends' happiness.

{ I don't miss him; I miss who I thought he was.

—unknown }

• Don't enable.

I know a girl named Teri, and she has a bad habit. She forgives people who hurt her, specifically the guys she has dated. I admit that part of this sounds very nice of Teri, except for one thing: the guys she forgives just do the same thing to her over and over. In other words, she's not really forgiving them; she just feels like she is. In reality, because they can't appreciate love and forgiveness, she is enabling them to continue using her.

Life isn't just about *your* intentions. If you are a girl and forgive a guy just so that you won't lose him, or vice versa, then he only gets the message that it's okay to wrong you.

It's because we hear behavior more than we hear words, and we respond to behavior more than words too. This is what *enabling* is, and any therapist can clearly define it for you.[1] Did your ex lie to you and you took him back? Well, guess what? Even though you are forgiving, he most likely learned that he can continue to lie to you and you'll take him back, with minimal effort. This is why people get trapped in relationships like this over and over and over.

Now . . . in a marriage, it's different. When people really join their lives together, even lying or cheating may be an issue to try to work through. There is more at stake in a marriage, and people should try to work through their conflicts, no matter what. But luckily for you, in a dating relationship you don't have to try to work through black-and-white things like that. Don't allow yourself to be treated poorly, period. Just don't—you don't have the time in life for it. The danger isn't just with the relationship you're in currently; it's also that you will develop a habit of accepting poor treatment. Adults who accept being treated poorly usually started that habit young. Habits are habits, good or bad.

• Don't bring basketball into it.

And why would I bring basketball into it anyway, Chad? Well . . . because it's an easy way to introduce rebounding—something great in basketball, and terrible for dating. *Rebounding* is emotionally moving to someone else too quickly after a breakup—and it doesn't work out well. I've found that the couple of times I've wanted to rebound with someone after a relationship, it's because it distracts me, simply put. It distracts me from having to think about the past, especially if I don't know what to do about it. Sometimes looking for a way to be distracted is fine. Reading a book, hanging with friends, and taking up a new hobby are all great distractions—we all know this. But it's not okay when you use someone romantically to distract you, because those people have hearts and feelings too.

More often than not you'll just end up comparing your new date with your ex and then feeling even lonelier and more confused than ever. You'll probably confuse the other person too, and most people don't need any more confusion, especially with details of the heart. Especially big on the "don't do" list is rebounding with your ex's friends, bestie, or bff. That's a lame and obvious move. And it has no place in mature relationships. Rebounds are for basketballs, not people.

❁ ❁ ❁

Sometimes it can be good to review the "don't do this" lists of life, mostly because of how much fun it isn't. But you should also know this: there are a few other potential roadblocks you need to know about on your path. They're kind of big ones, but don't worry, you can get around them.

So let's be positive and cheery about change. Life is really short, and we do only get one. It's not meant to be wasted in pain and confusion. I hope you feel good about this. I do. Okay . . . now for those "demons" you need to watch out for . . .

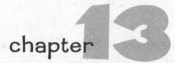

chapter **13**

DEMONS IN YOUR WAY

{ When things aren't adding up in your life, start subtracting.

—chad }

You are on a very important journey, and it will quite literally take you down a new path in your life, to a different life than the one you would have had. It happens because of decisions you're making right now, and I'm not just being dramatic. But here's the thing—and it's important enough to devote a complete chapter to—there are some big roadblocks in your way. Call them warnings, real big warnings, or something creepier, like demons. The word *demon* has many meanings, but one of them comes from the Greek verb *daiesthai*, and it means "to divide." When you decide you want to change the direction of your life, these demons, these "divisions," will try to stop you. So let's begin with super-sad puppies. I know, I know, that's a terrible sentence. I know.

SUPER-SAD PUPPIES

Have you ever been to an animal shelter? I've been a handful of times and have always loved going. But each time I've gone, I see something that kind of troubles me. There's always one dog that doesn't look like the rest. Not because it is has extra legs or three eyes or anything, but because it's usually lying there in the cage in a catatonic state. The last one I saw was a little beagle, a breed that can look a little sad and droopy anyway, so this one looked super extra sad. His extra sadness was making me sad too. Who wants to see an extra-sad puppy? Not this guy. I love dogs, and I love them more when they love me back. My counselor says this is fine . . . so don't make a big deal about it.

Sad Face the beagle was completely and utterly hopeless. He had given up and checked out of life—he just happened to still be alive, lying on a cement floor. Whether it was abandonment or abuse that caused him to be this way, he believed he was alone and in a cage and that no one would ever care for him.

Now replace your mental picture of this dog with a sixteen-year-old girl or guy. Picture them lying hopeless on the cold floor of a cage. Whether it's a person or a dog, any living creature without hope withers and slowly loses life. And you know what? There are millions of people in these "cages" of hopelessness. They aren't living their lives; they're just waiting for their lives to be done.

There are very, very few things more harmful to a person than hopelessness and believing you have no control over what happens in life. Here is the great news, though: people—unlike puppies—have opposable thumbs. If you don't know the striking difference between living life with an opposable thumb and life without one, then spend some time on Wikipedia. For this analogy, we could use those opposable thumbs to open the cage of hopelessness and walk out, for example. And if you feel that you are stuck in one of those cages . . . you are *not* alone. You do have people who care about you—whether you can see them right now or not.

I don't know what you believe about God, but I believe that God is love and love is God in a way we will never comprehend the vastness of. I believe that God loves you and me and everything in creation on a scale we can't even begin to fathom. Sometimes I'll browse through some of the images from the NASA Hubble telescope (and if you haven't looked at them, they're magnificent), and I'm reminded about a simple reality: look how much I don't know about this giant, amazing universe. I think it makes God even bigger, but it also makes sense of God in ways that we *can* understand—in goodness, sacrifice, love, kindness, and compassion. When I am up on a mountain looking around, I feel connected to God in a way that I'll never understand completely. I like the story of God and people and how much he loves us. It's a very beautiful story, and the most famous in the history of the world for a reason. I like that Jesus talked about truth and meaning and love, saying, quite famously, "You will know the truth, and the truth will set you free" (John 8:32). I like that my God tells me to search for the truth, and that is where freedom is.

{ "I have come that they may have life, and have it to the full." —Jesus in John 10:10 }

THE DEMONS THING

IF I WERE A DEMON

In 1 Peter 5:8, we are warned to be on the alert because "your enemy the devil prowls around like a roaring lion looking for someone to devour." See, if I were the enemy, I would use people's emotions against them. I would sabotage their emotions and make them fight a civil war within themselves. Why? Well, because it's our emotions—especially fear, shame, and blame—that are the real roadblocks in our journey to a better everything. Turns out, I'm not the only one who knows this. The devil is really smart. To move on with your life, you have to study these demon enemies, learn to recognize them, and fight them so that you can defeat them. So let's take a look at the first—and one of the biggest demon roadblocks—fear.

FEAR

Consider Alicia, a typical teenage girl. Alicia wants to know, "I have some problems with my boyfriend. Should I break up with him, yes or no?" A simple yes or no answer might help her in the short-term, but what

> Fear holds you back and love moves you forward.

happens when the next problem comes along? Alicia will need help finding an answer to that problem, as well . . . *unless* she learns how to figure things out for herself.

Here's where the fear comes in. Fear makes you doubt

your own abilities and resist change. Fear keeps you stuck in the same-old, same-old. To put it simply: fear holds you back and love moves you forward. Fear is the source of despair, depression, and hopelessness. But love—not to be mistaken for romantic love—is the source of deep joy, passion, kindness, innovation, change, redemption, forgiveness, acceptance, and hope. Don't get me wrong, fear is helpful at times. There's a reason getting too close to the edge of a cliff makes your knees tremble—that's healthy fear—but this is different. The same fear that keeps you from changing your life also keeps you away from the good stuff in life. Take Pete, for example.

Hey, Chad,

There is this girl I like, but I'm too shy to talk to her. I mean . . . almost a weird kind of shy. I don't know how to get to know her. Do you have any advice to get over my shyness?

—Pete

Is shyness something you can relate to? Because I sure did . . . and still do, on occasion. It's easy to read about fears like shyness and just kind of skim over them, but sometimes not dealing with even the small fears can keep us trapped in their cycle. For years. Fear is a hidden epidemic and always has been. Most people struggle with fear in some way. Just to give you some personal examples, I've jotted down some of the things that have been fear-driven in my own life.

Chad's Fears (Limited Edition)

- **That things won't ever work out for me:**
  A lot of my family has struggled with relationships, jobs, money, and dreams. I've had relationships end, very badly, in fact. So how can I ever say a single word about relationships to others? No matter how many books I write, or lectures I give, or places I travel . . . there's still the tiny voice in the back of my head that says, "Somehow these things will all go away, and you won't be happy or successful. Look at your whole family and all the struggles they go through. This is half of who you are."

- **That people will misunderstand me:**
  I can be a people-pleaser. It's difficult for me when people are upset with me.

- **That people won't understand my work:**
  I painstakingly concern myself with how I word things, connect things, and communicate the ideas I'm trying to get across. But sometimes I get trapped in my own fear of leaving something out or saying something wrong. I'm afraid that I'll be hurting or misguiding someone who needs help, and that I will fail them and then become a failure myself.

Let me tell you . . . sitting and thinking about your fears is illuminating. It's scary how many things we are scared of. But I would encourage you to write down a few of your own fears too . . . or not. But I hope you do. It's important to name them and get them out there. Why don't you try it right now?

_____

_____

_____

___ ___   ___

_____

Here's the thing you need to know about fear: very simply, it's fine to have it, and it's natural. But let it inform you, not guide you. So how do you do this? How are you supposed to actually get over real fears, face them, and conquer them? Well . . . you start by looking at things differently. They become a lot less scary when you look at things from different ways. Let's start with fearful little sayings that are dumb. Like . . .

YOU SHOULD BE ASHAMED OF YOURSELF
  Shame says, "Who do you think you are?"

  Freedom says, "I'm me, and it's pretty great.
  Thanks so much for asking!"

The sentence that says, "You should be ashamed of yourself" is one of the most harmful sentences in human history. I believe, along with lots of other professionals, psychiatrists, and other scientific-type smart people, that the root of many of the problems in our lives is a single thing: shame. *Shame itself is rooted in fear, and it can destroy you like a cancer from the inside out. And it can keep you from moving forward in life, and in relationships especially.*

Chad,

People don't think I see the way they look at me or the way they act around me, but I do, I just act like I don't. They look at me like I'm disgusting and repulsive, and I feel it every day. I feel when someone is staring at me with hate in their eyes. I can hear when someone says, "Ewww, here she comes. Why can't she just stay home?" as I walk by. It's getting really, really hard to just exist, Chad. I don't know what to do.

—Tiffany

Shame has been described as the "swampland of the soul," and Tiffany is drowning in this swamp. She is describing a feeling that everyone has at one time or another—that feeling that whispers, "You are not good enough." And this is poison to our souls.

Are there things that you've thought you aren't good enough for or good enough at? Try putting those things on paper here. Naming what you're fighting makes it easier to beat.

_____

_____

_____

_____

It's difficult not to compare everything we are and every-thing we do to someone else. Being smart, pretty, funny, tall, short, fat, or quiet is usually meant in comparison, as in "smarter than Jim" but "not as smart as Heather." And when we decide we're not as good as . . . that's when shame walks in. So why do we even make these comparisons at all? Why do we decide if we have value based on someone else? Why set ourselves up like that? The answer is because we want connection to other people.

Your life, my life, and everyone else's life is about being connected to people. People are what make this life worth living. So when we compare ourselves to others, what we're really asking is, "If someone really knew everything about me, even the bad stuff, would I be good enough for someone to like me, even love me?" That's where the demon called shame comes in.

One easy way to understand shame is to think of it as "the fear of disconnection." Shame is when we ask ourselves, "Is there something about me that would make me unworthy of being accepted by other people?" It's closely connected to an inferiority complex. Shame is universal—everyone has it. People who aren't capable of experiencing shame are called sociopaths . . . or brain damaged.[1]

GUILT IS NOT SHAME

Guilt and shame are often confused, but they are not the same thing. Here's the simple difference:

Guilt says, "I *did* something wrong."

Shame says, "I *am* something wrong."[2]

Guilt is healthy in the right doses. It's that feeling you have when you regret that you've done something wrong. Guilt focuses on your bad behavior ("I wasn't ready for a test"), while shame focuses on self ("I'm not good at tests and never have been"). Guilt wants to make things right. Shame says you are what is wrong and you can't be made right. Shame can lead to addictions, depression, violence, bullying, eating disorders, and even suicide. It's seriously bad stuff . . . the shame . . . not you.

SHAME: GIRLS VS. GUYS

Both guys and girls try to hide their imperfections. Do you do this? I do. I mean, it's good to try to better ourselves and all, but to try and hide our imperfections also hides what makes us unique and beautiful. After all, everybody is imperfect in some way, actually in lots of ways. But here's what I've learned as I've tried to deal with shame and the "Am I good enough?" demon . . . I actually like my imperfections more and more. I don't like trying to be perfect. I like to admit I'm wrong and that I don't always have to be right. It's a *huge* stress relief. I like my quirks and my odd little habits; they are what make me . . . me.

I've also discovered that shame affects guys and girls very, and I mean very, differently. Part of that is biology, but a lot of it is also sociology—the way our culture expects us to act.

Girls

For girls, shame usually revolves around the illusion of perfection—which is especially tough when you are constantly bombarded with messages about how imperfect you are. The illusion that perfection is possible is sold in every type of bottle and tube imaginable—from what to do about those "short, stumpy lashes" to "how to tone your abs in ten seconds."

The world shows you pictures of "perfect" girls (thank you, Photoshop) and tells you perfection is possible . . . and shame on you if you're not like them.

But it's not just physical image that girls try to perfect, it's also relationships, friendships, personal identity, life plans, and so on and so on. The problem is . . . perfection really isn't possible, and you'll just make yourself miserable trying to be perfect. Don't be ashamed of who you are—imperfections and all.

> "The LORD your God . . . will take great delight in you, he will quiet you with his love, he will rejoice over you with singing."
>
> —Zephaniah 3:17

Guys

For guys, shame centers mostly around one thing . . . whether or not you're seen as *weak*. Guys compare themselves with one another physically—who's the tallest, strongest, fastest, most "est" around. And if you don't come out on top of the pile, that's when the shame begins.

SHAME KILLS THINGS

Shame kills a lot of things, and one of those is relationships. It keeps us from being truly known by others. It makes us afraid to be vulnerable, to open up and let others see who we really are. Shame makes us try to hide our embarrassments, insecurities, fears, and disappointments. Here's the thing, though, and this is giant: it's only when we open up that we can *find* joy, creativity, belonging, and love. Shame not only causes bad feelings; it kills the good stuff too.[3]

THE CURE

I'm going to tell you something that's kind of heavy now, and it's the cure for shame. It's called courage, but it's not the laugh-in-the-face-of-danger kind of courage we typically think about. The word *courage*, when it first came into the English language, came from the Latin word *cor*, meaning heart. So courage originally meant "to tell the story of *who you are* with your whole heart." That means, very simply, that it takes courage to be yourself. It takes a willingness to be vulnerable and admit your mistakes and imperfections. People who are able to "tell the story of who they are with their whole heart" learn to do so openly, honestly, and wisely. Start small. Simply saying, "I was wrong," "I'm sorry," or "I don't know" is a huge step in the right direction. Courage includes sharing faults, weaknesses, and pain, just as Danielle does here . . .[4]

Chad,

I messed up and got pregnant by my ex-boyfriend. I feel like I won't be good enough for any guy because I'll always have that. I also grew up in a really broken home, and I've never felt like I'm good anyway. Please help if you can.

—Danielle

Danielle,

I appreciate your honesty about the things that have happened. That's not easy to do. So now I'm going to tell you something, and I hope you learn this now so that you never have to live again not knowing it: you are not a collection of your mistakes.

It's a waste of time to continue to feel bad about past mistakes you can do nothing about. So forgive yourself, friend; that is the answer. Forgive yourself, ask for forgiveness, be open and honest, and give quietness and prayer some heavy consideration. This is how you can learn to move on, to love yourself, and to keep your head held high. If you need to find a preacher, a friend, or someone else to help you through this process, then please do. God wants you to experience forgiveness. He wants great things for you, and this includes living a life without guilt and shame.

—chad

What Danielle might be struggling with is the idea of *grace*. God's grace is the most revolutionary concept in the history of the world. You are already loved . . . in spite of what you have done and in spite of all the mistakes you will ever make. God loves you infinitely more than you could ever imagine so much that he sent Jesus to die for your mistakes and to give you his grace.

BLAME

Blame is not just annoying; it's cancerous. It is not some little dart that stings; it's a poisonous spear. And when break-ups happen, blame usually comes knocking—or pounding—on the door. Blame comes in two flavors, which sounds like ice cream maybe, but is far less enjoyable. The two basic "flavors" of blame are *blaming self* and *blaming others*.

And just so you know, blaming is not complaining. It's very different. Professionals define blame as . . .

- a way to let out pain and discomfort.
- a way of devaluing others, resulting in the blamer feeling superior and blameless.
- a tactic of using repetitive behaviors, innuendos, and exaggeration (think "you always" or "you never") to manipulate others.[5]

THE BLAME GAME

Here are some simple examples of blaming, but there are millions of ways to do it.

☑ I only did it because you didn't _____ .
☑ I *only* want to make it better. She's the one causing the problem.
☑ If you hadn't done X and Y, then I wouldn't have had to do Z.

☑ This is your fault!
☑ You never_____!
☑ You always_____!

BLAMING OTHERS

When people blame others, they are either trying to eliminate blame for themselves or trying to wholly devalue someone else. When you blame someone, you are trying to define who that person is, what he or she does, and why it's wrong. Personally I really, really dislike it when other people try to define who I am, and I'm guessing you do too. I like taking care of that job myself. Blame is used as a way to dominate, define, and belittle people. It also allows the blamer to off-load their own guilt or shame while avoiding any responsibility for the same faults. Blamers often say they are just pointing out a mistake, but in reality, blamers are really saying, "You are wrong . . . and I am better than you."

SELF-BLAME

Here's another reason why people can't move on. There's another side to blame, another flavor, and one that's possibly even more harmful than blaming others . . . blaming yourself.

Sadly, self-blame often happens in cases of abuse and sexual assault—especially in young girls. Roughly one out of every four girls and one out of every six guys will be sexually assaulted in their lifetime. Psychologically, physically, emotionally, and literally for your brain, it's one of the most traumatizing and confusing things that can happen to a person—especially a young person. Victims struggle even to report the assaults, so that 54 out of 100 victims who experience sexual assault or rape don't tell the authorities, and this is why: self-blame.[6] Victims often feel that they are somehow responsible for part or all of the attack. Let's be very clear here: that is a lie, period. Yet victims often turn the blame inward on themselves instead of where it should be, toward the offender.

Self-blame isn't just limited to physical attacks, though. When people blame themselves for things that aren't their fault, it can cause them to develop a victim identity . . . and can lead to them being mistreated by others even more. To get all technical about it, the psychological profile of self-blame or victimization includes a pervasive sense of helplessness, passivity, loss of control, pessimism, negative thinking, strong feelings of guilt, shame, remorse, and depression.[7] Did you catch all that? Nobody needs that.

Self-blame is not something that can simply be swept under the rug. Because self-blame deals in delusion and shame as a way to process traumatic events, a thing called *cognitive reprocessing* is needed. That's a fancy way of saying rewire the brain. Therapists can help self-blamers "undo" their harmful ways of thinking, feeling, and processing life's events. If you're caught in a self-blame cycle, please reach out—there are people who can and will help you.

DEALING WITH BLAMERS

When dealing with blame from a breakup—whether you are the blamed or the blamer—here are some tips to put an end to the game:

- DON'T become defensive and validate the blame by arguing. Don't even argue about facts; blame is about feelings, not facts.
- DON'T assume there is a logical reason for the blame.
- DON'T assume that the person really believes what he or she is saying or always feels that way.
- DON'T assume that because the blame is inaccurate that the person is being deliberately manipulative or calculating. He or she may be so focused on feelings that behavior becomes irrational.
- DO remember blame isn't about you; it's really all about the way the other person feels.
- DO listen to the feelings being expressed rather than the facts. While the facts may be way off, the underlying feelings are often real: "I feel scared," "I feel worthless," "I feel weak," and so forth.
- DO respond with "I" statements, such as "I feel scared when you say that."
- DO remember that what the person is feeling is probably temporary. He or she will likely feel differently in a few days or a few hours.
- DO try to get the person to talk about the real issue . . . as long as you are able to do so without feeling threatened or hurt yourself.
- DO politely, briefly, and calmly state the truth *once and only once.*

✿ ✿ ✿

The only way to get rid of blame is to reject it and reject using it. There is a huge difference between blame and pointing out something wrong that someone did. If you need to point out something wrong to someone, figure out a way to do it that offers a solution and doesn't just leave that person feeling worse about it. That's called conflict resolution, and it tries to fix a problem. Blame is like taking a knife, cutting someone's leg, and then pointing out that the leg is bleeding. Blame is a knife, not a Band-Aid. Galatians 6:1 says you should help those who are doing wrong "gently." "Gently" does not involve knives . . . pretty sure about it too. Maybe more Band-Aids, less knives.

See Ya, Demons

Your job in life is not to be perfect. This means that when you mess up—and you will—you don't have to feel stupid or ashamed. Being imperfect means being human. You will have to struggle in your life, but struggle can be a good thing if you let it teach you. All personal growth comes from the struggle between "what is" and "what should be." At times you'll be confused, angry, depressed, sad, and embarrassed, but do *not* accept the feelings of fear, shame, or blame.

Fear, shame, and blame are the demons that want to knock you off the road of life. At their root, they try to find ways to tell you that you aren't good enough—either because of who you are or what you've done. Now, I can't speak for you, but I can speak for me, and I'll tell you this much . . . when I really believe that "I am enough," everything in my life changes. The thing is, I have to remind myself of this fact every day. Some days it's harder to believe it than others, but I'm going to get better at knowing this, and you will too. Because here is the truth, and it will never change:

You are *enough*, and you are worthy of being loved.

And the curious thing about love is this: when we feel worthy of love, we become free to start living in love. We are better able to give love and receive it. And I'm not just talking about romantic love here, but a love like God's love. A love that reaches out to family, friends, and fellow man and tries to make a difference in this crazy-weird world. You could do that, ya know. You really could.

chapter **14**

LONELY, SAD, LOVING, HAPPY

{ The stone which the builders rejected
has become the chief cornerstone.
—Psalm 118:22 NKJV }

It Will Be Okay

I'd like to tell you why it's going to be okay. In fact, no matter what happens, what has happened, or what will happen, everything will be okay. I don't know a lot of things, but I do know that.

{ Men's best successes come after
their disappointments
—Henry Ward Beecher }

213

Something that people don't always guess about me is that I don't always do well at talking about myself, in books especially. I don't know if you are supposed to say this as an author or not, but being a slight introvert, I always feel like stories about myself are just taking up other people's time. So it's fitting that I would wait until the last chapter. Either way, I'd like to tell you how Loneliness and Pain—once my enemies—have become my friends and have helped me tremendously.

PAIN AND MY QUALITY OF LIFE

{ I like the dreams of the future better
than the history of the past.
—Thomas Jefferson }

I'm not a mathematician, but it seems that if there were a simple math equation for life, then it might look something like this:

Good Stuff > Bad Stuff = Good Life

Bad Stuff > Good Stuff = Bad Life

In this equation, if we have way more good things in life than bad things, or good feelings than bad feelings, then we will be happier rather than sadder. In many ways this makes sense. I mean, seems like a decent goal for everyday life—laugh more and cry less. The thing is . . . I'm not sure if I believe that anymore, and I'm not sure that you should either. Just in case, ya know . . . you do.

Here is why: I have spent most of my life trying to avoid two things: Loneliness and Pain—mostly because they don't feel good, and I really don't like things that don't feel good. So it wasn't until I was forced to spend time with Loneliness and Pain that I realized two things. First, they are incredibly difficult, sad, hard, and miserable. And second, they're some of the best things that ever happened to me . . . and I mean it. Also, I should probably explain that.

The last couple of years have been the best and the hardest I've ever known—all at the same time. And can I just say . . . that's really confusing and weird. For a lot of the book, I have talked about learning what you can control in life and what you can't. And when I say that the only thing I can really control in life is myself, I believe it. We can't control other people's decisions. Period. This is just a fact, but when it gets "fact-ed" onto us . . . it doesn't feel good. So I was lonely and I was hurting for a while. This stuff happens sometimes, with no wonderful explanations. Life's funny like that sometimes.

I INVITED LONELINESS AND PAIN TO STAY

A while back, Loneliness and Pain decided to move into my life and become roomies. They were sticking around for a while, apparently, whether I liked it or not. Then . . . one day, something interesting happened. I got really annoyed at Loneliness and Pain, which is weird to say. Then . . . I got mad. So one night, I had a little "talk" with them, and it was admittedly a very odd moment, if you were a fly on the wall observing.

Mostly because I said out loud, verbally, to Loneliness and Pain (who are not human), "You know what, guys? I'm tired of being afraid of you, and I'm sick of trying to avoid you. If you really are gonna just be here for a while, then guess what? Take a seat and get comfy, pals, because we are gonna be great friends." And this very odd, personal moment in time is when something started to change.

It helped me. I figured I might as well try to learn from these things I've been trying to avoid. That decision quite literally has been changing my life ever since. For the first time in my life, when I felt lonely, I didn't just try to *stop* being lonely right away. I was going to make the best of a bad situation. I wasn't sure it would work, but I figured I would give it a shot. After all, the books and research, the doctors, advice from my friends, and tens of millions of people before me said that good things could come from bad situations. Then . . . it started to work. And . . . it was weird.

I read more. I talked way more about my feelings with friends (mostly because I knew it was a good thing to do, not because I wanted to). And then . . . people started to share their stories back with me. A lot. A whole lot. I learned new things about people I've known for decades. It turns out my confusion and rough patches in life are a lot like the ones other people have had; we'd just never had a reason to bring it up in conversation until then.

I processed my past, looked through my life experiences again, and examined my faults, honestly. It's good to know them and to be able to say them without shame. My imperfections don't define who I am; I just need to be more aware.

Slowly . . . I began to smile more. I listened to people more and empathized with their confusion in life. I also realized how important it is for people to feel encouraged. It meant the world to me when my friends encouraged me. So I figured it might mean a lot to other people too if I really started going out of my way to sincerely compliment and encourage others. It is amazing to watch what happens when you tell other people great things you think about them. And you know what? I found out that I really do *love* encouraging others. I really, really love it.

I could go on and on about all the things I learned in those few months that Loneliness and Pain moved in with me. But the simplest point is this: Loneliness and Pain gave me the best gifts I've ever gotten in life. They taught me about all of the good that comes from the terrible. I learned, from my actual experience, that smiles really do come after the sadness.

AIRPLANE MOMENTS

As I mentioned, life kept going. It has a way of doing that regardless of our feelings. I slowly started to replace the loneliness with new experiences in life. Some days were better than others, but it's called a *process* for a reason. Then one day . . . at an odd time in an odd place . . . I had a deep moment of personal clarity, if you will.

I was catching a flight to L.A. one evening, just as the sun was setting. I had put my earphones in and was listening to one of my favorite Icelandic bands. (And so what if they're the *only* Icelandic band I know; they're still my favorite.) I sat in my seat looking out the window, staring at the sunset as we took off over the ocean.

Then—in a moment like the ones you imagine in movies— it was like a couple of years of feelings and thoughts started flooding me all over, from everywhere. The thing is . . . they weren't bad feelings, but they were overwhelming for sure. And this is where I might start sounding all hippy-like . . . but it also happened in a leather seat with coffee while flying in the sky . . . so not that hippy-ish after all. I started feeling a random, deeply appreciative feeling for all the good things that had happened over the last few months. The new things, the change, and even the loneliness and pain. I became fixated by the beauty of all the simple things around me . . . the water and sun and clouds I was taking off into. I had just had a great conversation with my dad, I had good music in my ears, and my heart felt warm for the first time in a long time maybe, and in a new way. I felt incredibly thankful and emotional all at once. Then my mind started talking to me and saying . . .

I'm so used to flying I forget how beautiful these things I see are. This sunset is amazing, and I like that I can count on its coming and going every single day and night. I don't watch these sunsets enough, and I'm going to more from now on. And I am so used to technology, I forget about this music, this odd, amazing music, coming right into my ears, even though it was made somewhere far away in a room I've never seen. I am here with this sun and sky, and the tiny scratched reflectors on this piece of clear window, a half-inch thick, separating me from 400-mile-per-hour winds next to my face. I'm staring at the sunset while floating in the sky; that's incredible and strange and miraculous. Thanks, Wright Brothers, big shout out.

> O LORD, our Lord, how majestic is your name in all the earth! You have set your glory above the heavens.
> —Psalm 8:1

It's moments like those that I am trying to remember more often. I mean . . . there are a lot of really great things in life if I'll just remember to look for them. Happy people seem to appreciate the good stuff, and they seem to look for it a lot more. I may have difficult stuff happen in life, just like you, but there are always things to be really thankful for. For example: I have friends. Actually, I have really great friends from all over, and I really appreciate them. (Thanks, Luke, Kevin, Kirsten, Amy, Shack, Evan, Cindy, Kelly, Brian, Jim, Clint, Brad, and many others that better not be mad because they aren't on here—talk to my editor.) And I have had a best friend for over sixteen years. These are people who actually care about me. They like me. I know that now.

> Happy people seem to appreciate the good stuff, and they seem to look for it a lot more.

For me, it's important to remember moments like this one on an airplane . . . where this sunset-picture is happening, and that music is playing, and I'm crying a little, but it's kind of joyful and thankful, all mixed with tears. It was the first time I could imagine the whole laughing and crying at the same time thing that girls do. But then it disappeared again, sorry.

> If anything is excellent, or praiseworthy—think about such things.
> —Philippians 4:8

BAD . . . ISN'T ALWAYS BAD

It was difficult approaching a book like this one, with all these pretty heavy topics. But dealing with these things is the only way we can ever know ourselves, or other people, better. Yes, breakups and other tough things in life are painful. But they don't have to be *just* painful. They can be deeply good . . . if we will let them teach us. I think that's how God works too, or at least the mysterious part about God that I really like. People often ask, "If God is *so* good, why does he allow bad things to happen to good people?" And that is usually a very reasonable question, but it also paints a picture of pain and confusion and difficulty as only bad things. It's true bad things happen, but it doesn't mean great things can't come from broken ones.

What if the really difficult, sometimes confusing, sometimes painful things are also filled with lessons that can't be learned without them? What if we only grow by working through them the right way? What if "all things"—even the roughest stuff in life—really do "work together for good to those who love God" (Romans 8:28 NKJV)?

And here's an even bigger question for you: What if we really could, wholeheartedly, eventually say to the person who has *broken* our *heart*, "Thank you"? (Which absolutely does not mean you aren't allowed to cry and sob and snot all over yourself, because that happens too.)

When it comes to relationships, I think we forget how much we have to do with their outcome. Our choices matter, and they shape our lives. *Your* choices matter, and they shape your life. This much I know: In this life, you will go through confusion and hard times. You will most likely break up with people or have people break up with you. And in the end, it will be you who has to decide whether or not to move on through the hard stuff or to take it all with you. So my advice to you is this:

> If you are angry, be angry. You are allowed to be. But then ask yourself why, and try to understand it.

> If you are hurt, be hurt and feel the pain. It's there for a reason; you can learn from it.

> If you are sad and lonely, then you are sad and lonely. Don't try to instantly run away from it. Take time to work through it.

> If you're insecure, well . . . welcome to the club. There are millions of people just like you.

> If you are lost, don't panic. Just admit it, look around, ask for directions, and keep journeying on. It's okay to be lost; it's not okay to stay lost.

> Don't run away from the hard things in life. They are your teachers . . . if you will learn from them.

{ "For I know the plans I have for you," declares the LORD, "plans to prosper you and not to harm you, plans to give you hope and a future."
—Jeremiah 29:11 }

You are the main character in this story of your life. All the events and circumstances you face in life are the backdrop of your story, not the conclusion. And the best stories always involve struggle; it's how the characters grow. I hope you will write a great story, no matter what difficult things you face. And I hope that you will take every experience in your life, see it with open eyes, learn from it, and let it make you better. It is *your story*, after all. So keep writing, and always keep your head up.

All the best to you, my friend, in the great times and the difficult . . . especially in the difficult.

—chad

NOTES

CHAPTER 1

1. *Wikipedia, the Free Encyclopedia*, s.v. "Love," http://en.wikipedia.org/wiki /Love.
2. *Wikipedia, the Free Encyclopedia*, s.v. "Infatuation," http://en.wikipedia.org /wiki/Infatuation.
3. Chad Eastham, *The Truth About Dating, Love, and Just Being Friends* (Nashville: Thomas Nelson, 2011), 80–81.
4. 1 John 4:8.
5. Howard Halpern, *How to Break Your Addiction to a Person: When and Why Love Doesn't Work, and What to Do About It* (New York: Bantam, 1983), 249–253.

CHAPTER 2

1. *Wiki Answers*, s.v. "How Fast Does Earth Spin?," http://wiki.answers.com/Q /How_fast_does_earth_spin.

CHAPTER 3

1. *Merriam-Webster Online*, s.v. "Red Flag," Merriam-Webster, http://www .merriam-webster.com/dictionary/red%20flag.
2. Chad Eastham, *The Truth About Guys* (Nashville: Thomas Nelson, 2012); Chad Eastham, Bill Farrel, and Pam Farrel, *Guys Are Waffles, Girls Are Spaghetti* (Nashville: Thomas Nelson, 2009).
3. *Merriam-Webster Online*, s.v. "Dramatic," http://www.merriam-webster.com /dictionary/dramatic?show=0&t=1347576438.
4. "Warning Signs of Teen Dating Abuse," Oprah.com (2012), http://www.oprah .com/relationships/Warning-Signs-of-Teen-Dating-Abuse; Christa Miller, "Warning Signs of a Teenage Abusive Relationship," Livestrong.com (June 2010), http://www.livestrong.com/article/157552-warning-signs-of-a-teenage -abusive-relationship; American Psychological Association, "Teen Dating Violence Often Occurs Alongside Other Abuse," (February 2012), http://www .apa.org; "Living with Your Abuser," http://www.loveisrespect.org/get-help /safety-planning/living-with-your-abuser.

CHAPTER 4

1. Office for Victims of Crimes, "Stalking Victimization" (February 2002), www .ncjrs.gov/ovc_archives/reports/help_series/pdftxt/stalkingvictimization.txt.

CHAPTER 6

1. *Merriam-Webster Online*, s.v. "Make Up," http://www.merriam-webster.com/dictionary/make%20up.

CHAPTER 7

1. 1 John 4:8.
2. "Addiction Pain" (2006), http://addiction.readabout.net/addiction-pain.html.
3. Dr. Eric Berne, *Games People Play: The Psychology of Human Relationships* (New York: Penguin, 2009).
4. "Addiction Pain" (2006), http://addiction.readabout.net/addiction-pain.html.

CHAPTER 8

1. *Wikipedia, the Free Encyclopedia*, s.v. "Idiot," http://en.wikipedia.org/wiki/Idiot.

CHAPTER 9

1. Gay Gaer Luce and Julius Segal, *Sleep* (New York: Coward-McCann, 1966).
2. *Wikipedia, the Free Encyclopedia*, s.v. "Affective Science," http://en.wikipedia.org/wiki/Affective_science; *Wikipedia, the Free Encyclopedia*, s.v. "Affective Neuroscience," http://en.wikipedia.org/wiki/Affective_neuroscience.
3. R. P. Bagozzi, U. M. Dholakia, and S.Basuroy, "How Effortful Decisions Get Enacted: The Motivating Role of Decision Processes, Desires, and Anticipated Emotions," *Journal of Behavioral Decision-Making*, 16 (2003), 273–295.
4. *Wikipedia, the Free Encyclopedia*, s.v. "Autonomic Nervous System," http://en.wikipedia.org/wiki/Autonomic_nervous_system; *Wikipedia, the Free Encyclopedia*, s.v. "Emotions in Decision-Making," http://en.wikipedia.org/wiki/Emotions_in_decision_making.
5. James D. Fix, *BRS Neuroanatomy* (Board Review Series), Fourth Edition, (Maryland: Lippincott Williams & Wilkins, 2008), 177.
6. S. Han and J. S. Lerner, "Decision Making," in D. Sander and K. R. Scherer, (Eds.), *Oxford Companion to Emotion and the Affective Sciences* (Oxford: Oxford University Press, 2009), 111–113.
7. Melissa Hines, *Brain Gender* (New York: Oxford University Press USA, 2005).
8. A. Bechara, H. Damasio, and A. R. Damasio, "Emotion, Decision Making and the Orbitofrontal Cortex," *Cerebral Cortex* 10(3), (2000), 295–307, A. R. Bechara, H. Damasio, A. Damasio, and G. P. Lee, "Different Contributions of the Human Amygdala Ventromedial Prefrontal Cortex to Decision-Making," *The Journal of Neuroscience* 19(13), (1999), 5473–5481.
9. B. A. Mellers and A. P. McGraw, "Anticipated Emotions as Guides to Choice," *Current Directions in Psychological Science* 10(6), (2011), 210–214.
10. Yaling Yang and Adrian Raine, "Prefrontal Structural and Functional Brain Imaging Findings in Antisocial, Violent, and Psychopathic Individuals: A

Meta-Analysis," NIHPA (October 2009), http://www.ncbi.nlm.nih.gov/pmc /articles/PMC2784035/?tool=pmcentrez; D. S. Kosson, "Psychopathy and Dual-Task Performance Under Focusing Conditions," NCBI http://www.ncbi.nlm .nih.gov/pubmed/8772009.

11. Ibid.

12. Daniel Goleman, *Emotional Intelligence: Why It Can Matter More Than IQ* (New York: Bantam, 1995), 4–9.

13. "Rational Portrait of the Mastermind," Keirsey.com, http://www.keirsey.com /4temps/mastermind.asp.

14. J. Prinz, *Gut Reactions: A Perceptual theory of Emotions* (Oxford: Oxford University Press, 2004).

15. Daniel Goleman, *Emotional Intelligence*, 6–7; H. R. Pfister and G. Bohm, "The Multiplicity of Emotions: A Framework of Emotional Functions in Decision Making," *Judgment and Decision Making* 3(1), (2008), 5–17.

16. Daniel Goleman, *Emotional Intelligence*, 6–19.

17. Ibid., 3–142.

CHAPTER 10

1. *Wikipedia, the Free Encyclopedia*, s.v. "Frontal Lobe," http://en.wikipedia.org /wiki/Frontal_lobe.

2. Joe Dispenza, *Evolve Your Brain: The Science of Changing Your Mind* (Deerfield Beach, FL: HCI Publishers, 2007), 139–144.

3. Bethany Hamilton, "Biography" (2010), http://bethanyhamilton.com/about /bio.

4. Joe Dispenza, *Evolve Your Brain: The Science of Changing Your Mind*, 434.

CHAPTER 12

1. *Wikipedia, the Free Encyclopedia*, s.v. "Enabling," http://en.wikipedia.org/wiki /Enabling.

CHAPTER 13

1. Brené Brown, "Listening to Shame" (lecture online at TED Talks, March 2012), http://www.ted.com/talks/brene_brown_listening_to_shame.html.

2. Brené Brown, "The Gifts of Imperfection," (March 2011), http://www. ordinarycourage.com/my-blog/2011/3/4/the-gifts-of-imperfection-national -pbs-schedule.html.

3. Robert D. Caldwell, "Healing Shame: Understanding How Shame Bind us and How to Begin to Free Ourselves," http://www.psychsight.com/ar-shame.html (accessed July 11, 2012).

4. Ibid.

5. Brené Brown and Lauren Fortgang, *The Gifts of Imperfection: Let Go of Who You Think You're Supposed to Be and Embrace Who You Are* (Center City, MN: Hazeldon, 2010). (Also www.brenebrown.com; www.myordinarycourage.com).

6. Rape, Abuse, and Incest National Network, "Reporting Rates," http://www .rainn.org/get-information/statistics/reporting-rates.

7. *Wikipedia, the Free Encyclopedia*, s.v. "Blame," http://en.wikipedia.org/wiki /Blame#Self-blame.

ABOUT THE AUTHOR

Chad Eastham is a bestselling author and Revolve Tour speaker who writes and talks with young people everywhere. He has written numerous books, two educational DVD's, an award-winning health curriculum, and various articles about culture, faith, and social development for young adults.

When he's not a nomad, Chad makes his home in Nashville, but he still doesn't say "y'all."

ACKNOWLEDGEMENTS

To my dear friends and family, my family on the road, to my publisher and the researchers who diligently study these life subjects: I dedicate this book to the things I have learned from and with them.

I would also like to say thank you to all of the people who choose to love in life. People who are imperfect, flawed, hurt or happy, and yet still choose to love instead of fear. I have seen what the power of what love and encouragement does, and this has fundamentally changed me. So thank you once again for the reminder that love is the only thing that has ever changed the world. Even in the midst of our storms in life, there is still love.

And oddly . . . a special Thank You, to Pain and Confusion and Loneliness. I never wanted any of you, but would not become the person God intends me to be without you. I forever thank my Lord, Jesus Christ, who loved me and changed me forever, and uses all things good and bad to his benefit and glory.